AN
ENCYCLOPEDIA
OF
DESKS

AN
ENCYCLOPEDIA
OF
DESKS

MARK BRIDGE

SSP

A QUANTUM BOOK

Published by Shooting Star Press, Inc.
230 Fifth Avenue, Suite 1212
New York, NY 10001
USA

ISBN 1-57335-460-0

This book was produced by
Quantum Books Ltd
6 Blundell Street
London N7 9BH

Printed in Hong Kong by Sing Cheong Printing Co. Ltd

CONTENTS

INTRODUCTION

*An engraving
by Thomas Chippendale
the most famous cabinetmaker
of all time.*

Writing furniture made a late but dramatic appearance in the European domestic interior. Desks were only commonplace in churches, monasteries and palaces before the 17th century, yet by the middle of the 18th century a great variety was to be found in the homes of ordinary well-to-do people.

It is not difficult to appreciate that in medieval times, when life for the majority was close to subsistence level, reading and writing played a very small part in their lives. Those of noble birth lived in a way that was far from settled until the 17th century. The French word for furniture, *meuble*, is close enough to moveable/mobile to remind us of this mode of life. Thus furniture tended to be robust and functional except for pieces with symbolic value like thrones.

Furniture is recognised as a symbol of status in nearly all societies. Interestingly, writing furniture played no real part in the mainstream of this social code until the 18th century. In his Dictionary of the English Language, published in 1755, Samuel Johnson defined several forms of writing furniture, but the most basic is the desk, which he described as: 'An inclining table for the use of writers or readers, made commonly with a box or repository underneath it'. This seems to have been virtually the only piece of writing furniture found in homes before the middle of the 17th century.

Boxes of this kind remained a standard requirement of the traveller throughout the 18th and 19th centuries. They were made in all qualities, ranging from basic boxes to folding compendiums of presentation quality, featuring fold-out writing slopes, adjustable reading stands, inkwells, pounce pots, even candleholders. Although this simple medieval desk retained its own identity for centuries it was also one of the building blocks for the more complicated permanent writing furniture. Other major ingredients were rudimentary writing tables and small cabinets of drawers with flaps that let down. The only real precedent for large and fixed pieces of furniture for reading and writing was to be found in churches or monasteries.

By the time Johnson published his dictionary, itself a pointer to growing literacy in the community, the proliferation of desks shows that these skills of reading and writing were already much more important in the homes of the upper classes. The general development of writing furniture for the home in the 17th century was part of a widespread improvement in trade, communications and technical skills, and specifically cabinetmaking.

The new impetus was first evident in continental Europe. Tables solely intended for writing were to be found in Italian palaces in the 16th century; in the Low Countries compact writing cabinets seem to have appeared early in the 17th century. The new forms did not have much impact in Britain until the restoration of Charles II in 1660. By the end of the century a variety of different desk forms were in circulation in Europe and some had found their way to America. It is worth noting how the prototypes developed over the next two centuries.

Gateleg tables with fold-out flaps provided one starting point;

the flaps on some early examples formed a space in which to store writing materials when closed. Another early solution was to mount the simple slope-front desk on a stand and to put the hinges at the bottom of the flap so that it became a large flat writing surface when folded down and supported – an arrangement which is instantly recognisable as a prototype of the slope-front bureau. This form became standard well before 1700, as did the fall-front secretaire, where the flap remained vertical when not in use, hiding storage compartments, then creating a generous writing surface when opened.

These different forms of fold-away desk were developed in parallel with an essentially different form of desk, based on the table, where the writing surface was always on view. Writing tables of this kind enjoyed their greatest popularity in France, where the bureau plat, which had appeared in the late 17th century, took on fashionable features of the 18th and 19th centuries while remaining unchanged in practical terms.

The bureau Mazarin, a distinctive kneehole desk on legs characteristic of late 17th century French style, lost favour during the 18th century, but equivalent combinations of base drawers and large writing surface became standard library furniture in Britain, as the pedestal desk. Like the bureau plat, this type was ideally suited to more public rooms and was designed to stand in the middle of the floor space. In the 20th century, the flat-topped library table is the general model for the office desk.

In more intimate rooms fold-away desks (most fitted with locks) have nearly always been the favoured form, reflecting a concern for compactness and secrecy. The grand houses of the 17th and 18th centuries tended to be fairly public places and written documents became more vulnerable as literacy grew.

In England the firm preference was for the slope-front bureau with drawers underneath and often with a cabinet of drawers, or later a glazed bookcase, on top. There were many variations in size and design. The most striking are the large lacquer-decorated bureau-bookcases of the early 18th century, architectural in form and designed to stand against the wall. Such pieces are very different from the delicate little bureaux en pente favoured as ladies' desks in France at the same period. These were generally free-standing and raised on slender legs.

In 18th century America the combination of slope-front desk and bookcase was also the favourite form; an elegant echo of its generally more solid English counterpart. It became one of the most representative pieces of East Coast cabinet furniture, developing subtle but distinctive regional characteristics. This popular combination was adopted in Europe, though not in France. A distinctive Dutch form, with profuse marquetry decoration and a heavy *bombé* base with canted projecting corners remained popular throughout the 1700s, while German and Italian craftsmen developed fantastic rococo forms. The exagerratedly pot-bellied creations of the Venetians are hardly recognisable as kin to a more staid English equivalent.

The upright form of fall-front desk came back to favour in the second half of the 18th century, particularly in France, where it was known as a secrétaire à abattant. It lent itself to the more classical rectangular shapes which characterised the Louis XVI style and the French Empire style of the early 19th century. The same trends were evident in other countries and the vertical fall-front was the normal form on fold-away desks of the Biedermeier period in Austria and Germany from the 1820s onwards. Here too the emphasis was on bold shapes and large undecorated areas of plain veneer. The basic *secrétaire à abattant* forms a compact unit which can be adapted to fit many basic shells and which is unobtrusive when not in use, making it a favourite with 20th century designers struggling to escape traditional forms.

The large flat areas of these secretaires also present a broad canvas for decoration which has tempted designers of all periods.

A more modest 18th century development was the secretaire drawer, a feature made to look like any other drawer when closed, but which pulls out to become a fall-front writing compartment with pigeonholes at the back. Writing drawers of this kind were incorporated in all kinds of furniture. They became increasingly popular in Britain and America as the century waned and throughout the 19th century, as did the cyclinder front which more or less replaced the slope-front in France after the 1760s and became widespread in England and America.

During the 18th century France also took the lead in providing women with a great variety of well-thought-out smaller writing tables for everyday use. Very early the bureau Mazarin and its English and American counterpart, the small kneehole desk, seem to have served in the bedroom as dressing tables as well as desks. Small slope-front bureaux for ladies appeared on both sides of the Channel early in the 18th century, but the Paris *ébénistes* showed the greatest ingenuity and virtuosity in creating little *tables à écrire*. These were often work tables or delicate dressing tables, which also contained spaces for pen, ink, paper and a writing surface. No other writing furniture illustrates more clearly the importance of written communication in the pre-telephone era. Apart from these ingenious multipurpose pieces, the French also created the most distinctive and practical of all desks for women, the bonheur du jour. This enjoyed a great vogue among French ladies in the 1760s, was taken up all over Europe and revived many times.

The early 1800s saw several influential desk types emerge. In England the Carlton House desk, a stylish adaptation of the French bureau à gradin, was a Regency favourite and in the newly independent Federal America, tambour-fronted desks with fold-out writing flaps were fashionable and noticeably different from their counterparts across the Atlantic. The Davenport also appeared around the turn of the 18th century, a compact desk on chest immediately distinguishable from the slope-front bureau by being smaller, by the shallow angle of the writing surface and by the fact that the drawers are down the side. The first desks of this kind were seen in Britain in the 1790s, but they went on to become the typical item of writing furniture for the Victorian drawing room. In later models great ingenuity was used to pack in more features. The Victorian era saw many changes in the methods of furniture production. Rather surprisingly it was fashion rather than improved design that obsessed the new masters of the furniture trade, who revived one style after another.

One landmark in the 19th century was the patent desk manufactured in large quantities at the factory of William S. Wooton of Indianapolis. He created a closeable desk with over 100 drawers and pigeonholes. It was conceived on solid architectural lines and would be decorated according to the customer's pocket. Wooton's desk was practical and popular, but it also represents one of the dead-ends of High Victorian furniture design. The road to the office of the mid-20th century doubled back to reassess the styles and values of much earlier craftsmen.

It was the Arts and Crafts Movement that actually led to the manufacture of simple, practical furniture that was an honest reflection of labour-saving production methods. The medieval inspiration of the Arts and Crafts pioneers produced some clumsy writing furniture, for of course there were no real precedents for domestic desks from that age, but in general terms their thinking influenced younger designers.

In America, the architect Frank Lloyd Wright was one of the most important of the new generation. He commissioned deceptively simple oak furniture to complement many of the private houses he designed. When he designed metal office furniture for the Larkin Building in Buffalo, New York in 1906, Wright was also setting the style for the mid-20th century workplace. Designers, free of classically-inspired styles for the first time since the Renaissance, have explored the possibilities of plywood, plastic and tubular steel.

In the office other technological advances, like the typewriter and the telephone, have tended to dictate simple flat surfaces with drawers beneath, especially as this form was suited to the trend towards clean, efficient design.

Having considered a few of the different types of desk developed since the 17th century, it is worth considering the sources of information on the styles and conventions of the past.

People generally take little conscious note of the furniture fashions that are evolving around them, yet everyone carries with them a sense of what is 'modern' and what is outmoded. This presents no particular problem when talking about the 20th century, but the student of furniture history has to try to recreate a picture of evolving style from contemporary writing. Unfortunately commentators often ignore those commonplace details which would be of most interest, so that it is necessary to fall back on inventories of the contents of great houses.

Paintings and engravings are another good source of information, but the most influential sources have been the furniture pattern books issued for the guidance of householders and furniture makers. These can usually be taken to reflect what was fashionable. By far the most famous is the *Gentleman and Cabinet Maker's Director*, published in 1754 by Thomas Chippendale. Chippendale's *Director* differed from earlier pattern books in that he intended it as a trade advertisement, showing potential customers what his firm could provide. His advertisement must be one of the most successful of all time for his name dominates our view of a whole period of furniture history in Britain and America.

Pattern books and other specialised trade publications also highlight the problem of changes in the use of words. The word *bureau* is one of the most difficult in this respect. In France it is used to cover all types of writing furniture; in Britain today it is taken to refer to the traditional slope-front desk on chest already mentioned; Sheraton used it in that sense at the beginning of the 19th century; but half a century earlier Johnson had defined a bureau as a 'chest of drawers', a sense which it retains in the United States. In many cases these difficulties can be circumvented by simple and accurate description, but some terms are used in specific contexts in reference books and sale catalogues and most of these are listed in the glossary.

The illustrations in this book have been grouped in centuries to give a basic chronological sequence, but the ends of the chapters do not necessarily indicate abrupt changes in form or fashion. Furniture evolves continually and ideas take time to travel from one country to another and provincial areas always tend to lag behind the centres of fashion. It is possible to get some idea of the range of writing furniture in a given period, and these are the styles and examples explored in this book.

BEFORE

1600

Saint Jerome in his Study, a copper engraving by Albrecht Dürer, dated 1514. Early paintings and etchings are often a valuable aid to the furniture historian, since actual examples of furniture dating from this time are rare indeed. Here we are given a tantalizing glimpse into the study of a learned and pious man, seated on a simple stool with his writing slope resting on a table.

European writing furniture dating from before the 17th century is relatively rare. There are obvious reasons for this: not much was needed for the few literate members of society, and the likelihood of these few pieces surviving in any numbers is small. Certainly there is no evidence of the combination of cabinet, chest, bookcase and desk in a single convenient unit that appeared in the late 17th century.

To find the most common and substantial survivals it is necessary to look in places where reading and writing were accepted as part of everyday life and, from the fall of the Roman Empire onwards, these were churches and monasteries.

Not only were medieval churchmen more commonly able to read and write than the rest of the population, they also enjoyed a status that to some extent separated them from the hurly-burly of everyday life, allowing them to maintain libraries which would have been out of the question even for the lay gentry, who were frequently caught up in wars and internal power struggles.

The continuity of life in religious orders has meant that a good deal of ecclesiastical furniture has survived. The simple lectern, a book slope on a tall stand intended for reading aloud from the scriptures, remains a symbolic and practical item in churches today, but it was essential as a support for massive and heavy early books.

This practical use of the slope with a supporting ledge along the bottom edge influenced desk design right into the 20th century. It is to be found in more massive form in monastic settings, often as fixtures in libraries, and examples with panelled bases show great affinity with the later slope-front desks, except that they did not allow room for the knees of anyone who wished to sit at them and write.

Renaissance and earlier depictions of scholarly gentry or saints in their studies often show them at a bookstand on a pillar with a pen in one hand and an ink pot in the other while weights sometimes prevent the leaves of the book from turning over. Alongside this precarious and inconvenient arrangement one also sees illustrations of the more practical low table desk in use, which allows papers and books to be spread around.

While books remained rare and expensive, private libraries were few and large writing desks seem to have been absent from the homes of even the most rich and powerful. Palaces were furnished to impress and to reinforce existing degrees of precedence. State beds with luxurious hangings and the tiered buffets for the display of valuable possessions laid out on coverings of expensive textiles held a significance above the uses of everyday life and were more important to the career of a public figure than a show of scholarship.

In the largely public atmosphere of a court which was fre-quently moved around, small writing boxes seem to have been the rule, intricately fitted with all the necessities like ink and pens. Some, like the magnificently decorated sloping box of drawers and compartments made for Henry VII of England in about 1525, which survives in the Victoria and Albert Museum, were luxury objects; others were more utilitarian.

It was with the development of smaller private chambers in great houses that the appearance of the domestic folding desk was most intimately connected. As Renaissance ideas spread North through Europe from Italy, private scholarship became fashionable and the nobility aspired to closets or studies. The Renaissance man collected natural curiosities, as well as coins, medals and books which created a need for somewhere to store and study them.

By the late 16th century the fashion had reached Britain. The Oxford English Dictionary records an observer writing in 1586: "We doe call the most secret place in the house appropriate to our studies . . . a closet." To furnish their closets and to store the valuable curios, the new humanists could not turn to the Greeks and Romans for inspiration as they had set no precedent for cabinets of drawers or writing desks in their rather sparsely furnished interiors, where many objects were simply hung up on the wall or placed on open shelves when not in use.

The lack of direct precedents must certainly have been a factor in the rather tardy development of writing furniture. A great deal of medieval furniture made use of architectural conventions – pillars and arcading were common elements in chests and chairs – and this tendency was reinforced during the Renaissance, a movement largely fired by a new awareness of classical architecture. The results were often correspondingly massive, and not really suited to small and private chambers.

One source for the small and decorative writing cabinets that first appeared in Continental Europe in the 16th century was the East. The colourful lacquered cabinets of drawers behind double doors that became so popular in the following century were intricate and easily portable and may well have been a model for Western craftsmen at quite an early date.

Some of the earliest chests of small drawers with a single flap that fell forward and could be used for writing (as opposed to doors) came from Spain. These rectangular travelling cabinets, known as *vargueño* from the 19th century onwards, came into use in the 16th century. They were often plain on the outside, apart from elaborate clasps, but tended to be luxury objects with extravagantly decorated interiors showing a strong Moorish influence.

The banks of small drawers and cupboards were often arranged like architecture in miniature, but emphasis on concealed intricacy of this kind is characteristic of much of the writing furniture of later periods.

PRE-1600

1. An Early Medieval Table Desk

It is made of faded hardwood, with a carved top about 10in (25cm) square, set at a gentle slope on turned baluster legs, which are joined by stretchers with further small turned columns along each side. This well-made and rare survival from the Dark Ages is known as *Le Pupitre de Sainte Radegonde*, following traditional belief that it belonged to Radegonde, wife of Clotaire, King of the Franks in the mid-6th century. Radegonde forsook the corrupt life of the royal family and founded the Sainte Croix monastery at Poitiers, where the desk is still preserved. Whether or not it belonged to a saint, this is a good example of an early desk of the type seen in prints and paintings of the Middle Ages and the Renaissance. Like most early desks it has an ecclesiastical origin, emphasised here by the carved decoration: the Lamb of God at the centre, with the symbols of the four evangelists in the corners, Latin crosses to each side, a Maltese cross at the bottom and Christ's monogram at the top. The underparts, which are of mortice and tenon construction, are decorated with chevron bands and rows of dots and circles.

2. A Small Table Desk

It is 1ft 4in (41cm) wide and is thought to have been made for Henry VIII of England in the 1520s. Here the sloping lid has been thrown back and the front dropped down to reveal the painted and gilded decoration of the interior. The inside of the lid is embellished with looped strapwork containing the badges of Henry and his first wife, Catherine of Aragon. The inside of the front flap bears portrait medallions of 'Paris de Troy' and 'Helen de Greci' and opens to reveal three drawers, the centre one divided by partitions and the other two fitted with sliding lids. There is a further small partitioned drawer in the bottom of the righthand side. The desk is now covered on the outside with shagreen and mounted with gilt metal, work which dates from the early 18th century.

Small table desks seem to have been the favoured form of writing surface until the 17th century, and this is a fine example of sumptuous work befitting a royal palace.

3. A detail of the Henry VIII table desk,

with the second lid thrown back to reveal two lockable compartments with lids. The one at the back bears a medallion of the head of Christ and the one on the right depicts St George with the slain dragon at his feet. The inside of the lid bears the coat-of-arms of Henry VIII supported by two putti with trumpets, flanked by the figures of Mars on the left and Venus with Cupid on the right. This highly sophisticated piece of furniture shows a strong Renaissance influence and may have been the work of a foreign craftsman working in England.

4. A Late 16th-Century Inlaid Oak Table Desk

This is an English piece, fitted on the inside with a nest of eight drawers and with an old iron lock and the original strap hinges. The bog oak and light wood decoration is inlaid in the true sense of the term (that is, let into grooves cut into the solid carcase rather than laid on as a patterned veneer) and continues right round the box in a series of stylised palace façades and abstract geometric motifs. The form of this slope-front desk is typical, with a moulded ledge along the front edge to prevent books from slipping off. It is 2ft 3in (69cm) wide.

5. A Spanish 16th-Century Painted and Partially Gilt Vargueño

This 3ft 6in (1.48m) wide example has a chest base with a pair of drawers over a pair of cupboards, rather than the more commonly-seen trestle base. Behind the fall front there are 12 small drawers grouped around a cupboard with three more drawers inside. Notice the shell-fronted lopers pulled out to support the writing surface.

1

4

2

3

5

1600 TO 1700

A portrait of a gentleman in an interior by the 17th-century Dutch artist Gerard Ter Borch. He is working at a simple slope-front table desk with a leather-lined top and a lockable lid. Portable writing boxes have always been popular with travellers, but they seem to have been the commonest type of writing furniture in the home before the mid-17th century when larger permanent desks began to appear.

Visitors to large stately homes often remark upon the scant privacy that the finely decorated interconnecting rooms afforded their wealthy creators. The arrangement of successively grander rooms in long suites with a bedchamber at the end, makes the modern observer uneasy, not to say uncomfortable, for it is hard to imagine everyday life carrying on in such showy surroundings.

This luxurious discomfort may seem incongruous but it results from social rather than practical considerations. In the 17th century the standard arrangement of rooms in these large houses imitated the layout of Royal palaces.

As his medieval forbears had done, a king held state in a room equipped with a massive ornamental bed, but he did not necessarily sleep there. This bed chamber was approached through a series of ever grander rooms to which members of the court were admitted according to their rank on state occasions.

Such formal public life was seen at its most developed at the Château of Versailles, conceived as the embodiment of Louis XIV's wealth and power. His magnificent apartments, decorated in the 1670s, set him at the head of a visible chain of precedence. Even the furniture had a ritual importance, with some chairs for sitting on and others for show, and a range of conventions which governed who was entitled to sit down and those who had to remain standing on State occasions.

Louis XIV's example was followed all over Europe and not just in Royal palaces. Noble families with country seats had to emulate court practice if they wished to entertain on a grand scale and, because it is so well documented, it is worth looking at the arrangements at Ham House on the Thames outside London. It was altered and refurbished in the 1670s, after its owner, Countess Lauderdale, had visited Paris. Following the European style, suites of rooms were provided for the Duke, the Duchess and visiting royalty so that correct etiquette could be observed.

It was the showplace of an ambitious couple, where richly decorated collecting cabinets were on view, but nothing so practical as a writing desk appeared in the state rooms. To find the real living quarters in such houses it is necessary to look behind the scenes where one finds a growing concern for privacy and convenience. As at Versailles, beyond the farthest, grandest chamber in each suite at Ham there is a closet, a small place of retirement where the formalities of public life could be relaxed.

Such chambers had been provided for important guests at a much earlier date, but at Ham the Duchess created more than a bolt-hole. She had two adjoining private rooms, double-glazed against the cold and connected by back stairs to a bathroom.

The inventories of the time indicate that these were rooms for informal gatherings – tea parties are intimated by the "Indian furnace for tee garnished wt silver" listed here in 1679.

Also listed at the same time are two writing desks, one in each room, and another in the Duke's closet. There is no writing furniture at all mentioned in the 1645 inventory.

The desks themselves, described as 'scriptors', were small and simple cabinets on stands, filled with little pigeonholes and drawers. They were beautifully made, probably in Holland, with veneers of oystered kingwood, set off by small silver handles and mounts, but they are among the least overtly showy pieces in the house. They represent the innermost sanctuary within an already private room. The French word *secrétaire* draws attention to this idea of the desk as a place where papers and possessions can be locked away and kept secret.

The large double-domed bureau-cabinets which began to appear in Britain and Holland at the end of the 17th century and became standard items of furniture in the early years of the following century seem a long way removed from the diminutive scriptors, especially when they dominate the room with mirrored doors and brightly coloured lacquer decoration. They do, however, fulfil the same role and when opened out their size makes them almost closets in themselves. They represented a personal domain to which a gentleman could retire to sort out his affairs, even in a large room frequented by family and servants.

It was not only a desire for increased comfort in the home that brought about the great increase in the amount of writing furniture available by the end of the century, increased trade and improved postal services played their part.

The Low Countries provided a great deal of the expertise in furniture construction which enabled Britain to begin to catch up with the rest of Europe after the restoration of Charles II in 1660. The interior scenes of painters like Vermeer and de Hooch are filled with comfortable, practical furniture appropriate to a settled bourgeois lifestyle and Dutch craftsmen were ready to furnish the homes of the increasingly wealthy middle classes in other countries.

The influx of skilled labour to Britain was swelled by religious persecution elsewhere in Europe. When the Protestant William of Orange replaced the Catholic James II on the throne of England in 1688 many fine craftsmen followed the new king from Holland, for it was only three years since Louis XIV had revoked the Edict of Nantes, ending the religious freedom that protestants had enjoyed in France since 1598 and forcing many to flee the country.

France itself had benefited from the skills of Flemish and Italian craftsmen, particularly in the setting up of the *Manufacture Royale des Meubles de la Couronne* at Gobelins on the outskirts of Paris in the 1660s. Here Louis XIV sponsored workshops that not only provided the interior decoration for his ambitious palace-building programme, but also produced future generations of native craftsmen of the highest calibre.

As far as furniture was concerned, the great skill which was being perfected during the 17th century and which was effectively exported to Britain only after the Restoration was veneering. The rediscovery of veneering, a technique that had been known to the Ancient Egyptians, Greeks and Romans, brought about a revolution in furniture design. It made possible the building of substantial pieces of furniture without recourse to the frame and panel methods that tended to make earlier furniture ponderously heavy, and it allowed craftsmen to make the best possible decorative use of the beautifully figured hardwoods that began to arrive in Europe as world trade developed.

Ebony seems to have been the first hardwood sawn into thin sheets and applied to the surface of a carcase with glue, and the French term for the new generation of craftsmen, *ébéniste*, remain, although ebony ceased to be a widely-used veneer.

In Britain and America the new craftsmen were called cabinetmakers, a term which comes closer to suggesting the advances that the new technique made possible. Veneers could be cut into patterns that showed off the natural grain; they could be formed into naturalistic pictures (marquetry) or geometric designs (parquetry), but above all they covered all the joints in the carcase work, so that makers were free to attempt new forms.

Many of the desk forms found at the end of the 17th century can be seen as part of the experimental process that produced the more assured and practical writing desks of the 18th century.

6. An Early 17th-century Spanish Walnut Vargueño

This example has a trestle stand and a fitted interior of drawers and cupboards. The fall front is supported on lopers in the stand when lowered. It is 3ft 9in (91cm) wide. Though the complex pierced hinges, locks and fittings are typical of these distinctive Spanish pieces, the overall plainness of the exterior reflects the origins of the vargueño as a travelling chest. The interiors, however, are generally much more decorative and reflect the Moorish influence of the time. Intricate geometric designs are often built up from small pieces of ivory, ebony, tortoiseshell and other inlays. Trestle stands, known as *puentes,* are most common, but chest bases are also found, and the vargueño would seem to be the earliest form of the fall-front secretaire that was to become popular all over Europe in later centuries.

7. An Early English 17th Century English Carved Oak Table Desk

Fitted with an external bookrest and a shelf and two drawers beneath the lid, this desk is carved at the sides with triangular panels of vine leaves and bunches of grapes above a frieze of carved roses and lozenges. Carving was the principal method of decorating English oak furniture up until the end of the 17th century, when the crafts of veneering and lacquering were introduced from the Continent. It was also during this period that table desks of this type began to be incorporated as the tops of larger and more permanent bureaux with chest of drawer bases. This example is 2ft 1in (63.5cm) wide.

8. An American Oak and Pine Bible Box of the Mid-17th Century

1ft 11in (58cm) wide, it is carved along the front with a series of rosettes and scratched with the initials AG and the date 1644. It stands on turned maple feet. Simple table boxes with hinged lids for the storage of books and valuables were the nearest things to desks to be found in American homes before the end of the 17th century.

7

10

9. An American Carved Oak Desk Box, c1670

The box is only 14¼in (36cm) wide, with a sloping pine lid. The sides are carved with leafy branches and the initials *MF*. This rudimentary table desk has been attributed to Thomas Dennis or William Searle; both craftsmen worked in Ipswich, Massachusetts in the second half of the 17th century producing finely carved, joined furniture. Such pieces would have been used for storage, but the slant lid meant that they were also useful for reading and writing.

10. The Oak Writing Table Made for Samuel Pepys's Library in London

It is possible that 'Simpson the Joyner', who made bookcases for Pepys's Library, also made this writing table. The desk top, 5ft 5in (1.65m) wide and carved with moulding to match the bookcases, is supported on massive twin pedestals which are actually glazed bookcases intended to house Pepys's largest volumes. Pedestal desks did not become standard furniture in English libraries until the 1720s.

1600-1700

11. An English William and Mary Slope-Front Bureau in Oak

The way in which the top overlaps the gateleg base is typical of such desks, and a similar arrangement is found on many late 17th century examples with chest of drawer bases. The two centre front legs, which are neatly recessed into the body when closed, swing forward to support the writing surface. Inside the desk there are shelves, four drawers and a storage well, and three small drawers in the frieze provide additional storage space. After years of standing on damp floors, the feet of old pieces of furniture are often the first things to suffer, and on this desk some of the feet have been replaced.

12. An English William and Mary Black Japanned Kneehole Desk, c1695

This desk is decorated with a variety of Chinese-inspired scenes and stands on unusual bell-shaped feet. One of a pair, the desk has a single long drawer above a kneehole containing a cupboard and a small drawer, with three more small drawers on each side. Japanning, the imitation of Oriental lacquer work by European craftsmen, became popular in Britain in the late 17th century and remained an exotic, and expensive, form of decoration well into the 18th century. It is 2ft 11in (89cm) wide.

13. An English Late 17th- or Early 18th-Century Writing Chest

The whole desk is japanned in black and gold with chinoiserie landscapes and birds. The hinged top folds forward to form a lined writing surface supported on gatelegs which swing out from the body of the chest. The base has a concealed compartment with three drawers below, flanked by cupboards containing drawers and pigeonholes. This is an interesting hybrid combining the features of a bachelor's chest and an early gateleg desk. It is 3ft (92cm) wide.

16

13

12

11

14

15

14. An English William III Mulberry Wood Bureau, c1700

It is 3ft (92cm) wide, with two short and two long drawers below a writing compartment fitted with drawers, pigeonholes and a well. (This was a space used for storage found under the writing surface which doubled as a lid.) By the end of the 17th century the distinctive form of the English slope-front bureau was well established. This example, with its contrasting burr veneer and pewter stringing, is very much in the manner of Coxed & Woster, cabinetmakers who set up in business at The White Swan, St Paul's Churchyard, London, around the turn of the century. They are two of the best-known makers of their period, simply because they were among the few who labelled their work; several examples of different sorts of writing furniture bearing their name have survived. The pewter inlay with crossbanded veneer and the crossbanded framing around the sides of the pieces show the influence of Gerrit Jensen, the leading cabinetmaker of the period, who introduced such decorative elements to England from France in the late 17th century.

15. An English William and Mary Double-Domed Bureau Bookcase

This piece is 3ft 5in (1.04m) wide, with mirror-panel doors and is decorated with gilt chinoiserie scenes on a red ground, and topped by five silvered flower-vase finials. The base of two short and two long drawers also incorporates a hidden well beneath a slide in the writing compartment and there are candleslides in the upper section beneath a fully fitted interior of pigeonholes, drawers and cupboards.

16. An English William and Mary Marquetry-Decorated Writing Cabinet

This piece is 3ft 4in (1.02m) wide. The base is of two short and two long drawers beneath a fall-front writing compartment containing drawers and pigeonholes arranged around a central cupboard. There is a further concealed drawer with a cushion shaped marquetry front in the frieze just below the overhanging cornice. Fall-front desks of this kind are often referred to as escritoires today, but might have been known to their first owners as scrutoires. They were fashionable in the late 17th century, but seem to have been generally superseded by the bureau-bookcase in England early in the following century. Luxuriant floral marquetry of this kind is also typical of the period, inspired by the veneering skills of immigrant craftsmen from Holland and France.

17. A French Louis XIV Boulle Bureau Mazarin

This is a typical design, 5ft 2in (1.58m) wide, with a pair of pedestals containing three bow-fronted drawers each and a single frieze drawer in the centre. It is veneered on almost every surface with a brass-on-ebony design of fanciful scrolling foliage with swags, birds, figures, flowers, vases and other motifs. This distinctive style of late 17th-century decoration is often called *bérainesque*, a reference to the French architect and designer Jean Bérain, who worked with Charles-André Boulle and was one of the principal creators of the Louis XIV style. Bérain's fantastic populated scrolls are regarded as precursors of rococo decoration, but his designs always remain balanced and symmetrical. The usual brass, here combined with ebony and tortoiseshell, was by no means the only material used for decorative effect, although this became the favourite when the boulle technique was revived in the 18th and 19th centuries.

18. A Louis XIV Bureau Mazarin

This unusually large example, 5ft 11in (1.8m) wide, is veneered in kingwood and inlaid with pewter on ebony grounds. Most bureaux Mazarins are much smaller and serve as simple pedestal desks without fitted writing compartments, but this example is of a type that was popular in England and Holland as well as in France during the late 17th century. The rectangular top, with a large central medallion of pewter strapwork against ebony, is hinged down the middle and folds back to reveal a secretaire compartment. The top drawers are dummies which fold down to form the front of the writing surface. Both flaps are locked shut by means of two locks which are placed, rather unusually, between the simulated frieze drawers. Inside, the fittings are rudimentary compared with the many-drawered writing cabinets of the same period, having only three pigeonholes extending back under the rear part of the top. The decoration of the interior is particularly fine, however, with a marquetry coat-of-arms flanked by flowers and pewter and ebony monograms beneath coronets on the underside of the flap, and similar panels inlaid in *contre partie* on the writing surface.

17

20

18

19

19. A Boulle Marquetry Bureau

Not all magnificent furniture is easy to attribute or even to date. This mother-of-pearl, brass and stained shell boulle marquetry bureau had been stored in an attic at Knole Park in Kent, disregarded for many years before it came up for auction in 1987 and sold for £1.21 million.

The bureau is 2ft 11in (89cm) wide and 4ft 1in (1.25m) high including the upper section of three drawers, which are inlaid across the front with chinoiserie groups symbolising Astronomy, Painting and Geography, and at each side with a sculptor and a stone cutter.

The flap is inlaid with a landscape filled with courtly chinoiserie figures and a host of mother-of-pearl birds, and is lined on the inside with blue morocco leather. The interior holds a stepped arrangement of seven drawers in purpleheart above a walnut-lined well.

The base has a serpentine front in three parts, inlaid with five musicians in the centre and two rather puzzling garden scenes at each side. There are two small drawers at the bottom of the centre section and, on each side, a small drawer over a cupboard disguised as drawers and containing a kingwood *coffre fort* with a hinged top and a concealed drawer. The sides of the body are also decorated with garden scenes. The back is flat, indicating that it was intended to stand against a wall.

So unusual is the overall jewel-like effect that the origin of the bureau remains as mysterious as the distant dreamy scenes which cover it. As craftsmen travelled from court to court and no inventory entry for this or the only other similar known piece has turned up, present attributions range from a late-17th century Paris workshop to a South German one, c1720.

20. A French Louis XIV Bureau Mazarin

This bureau in the manner of André-Charles Boulle, with fruitwood and pewter marquetry, 3ft 9¼in (1.15m) wide, is supported on the capped tapering legs with curved X-stretchers typical of this type of desk. This example also has the usual cupboard in the back of the kneehole recess, as well as the less common lockable writing compartment beneath the hinged top. The rosewood and fruitwood veneered interior is secured by means of a single lock at the centre of the frieze, which drops flat in use. This arrangement provides only limited space for paper storage and fell from favour with the bureau Mazarin by the early 18th century.

21. A French Louis XIV Ebony Bureau Plat

This bureau is of massive design, with heavy ormolu mask and rosette mounts along a shaped frieze without drawers. The rounded rectangular top, 5ft 6in (1.68m) long, is supported at the corners on four female masks, a feature found on the early bureaux of makers like André-Charles Boulle and Charles Cressent. The bureau plat began to appear in French interiors in the late 17th century, and early examples show the monumental style of the period.

22. A French Louis XIV Boulle Bureau Plat

It is 6ft (1.83m) wide, with a rectangular leather-lined top, three frieze drawers and heavy cabriole legs with scrolled leaf toes. The inlay is in *première partie* with brass on an ebonised ground, and mounted with large masks at each end and on the corners. It is not possible to assign this high-quality desk to a particular workshop, for like many late 17th or early 18th-century pieces it is unmarked. None of the products of the workshop of André-Charles Boulle himself was marked, although this desk shows many similarities to a drawing thought to be by him. Work of this quality would only have been commissioned for palaces and great houses, in which the bureau plat was already becoming a standard item of furniture by the late 17th century.

21

22

1700
TO
1800

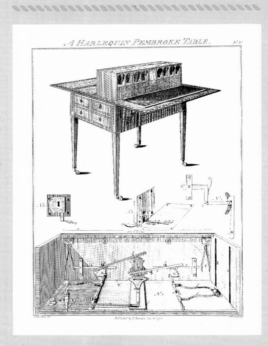

Sheraton's drawing for a Harlequin Pembroke Table in The Cabinet-Maker and Upholsterer's Guide of 1793, which he explains, '. . . serves not only as a breakfast, but also as a writing table, very suitable for a lady.' Sheraton delighted in complicated mechanisms and a long description accompanies the 'improved plan of the machinery' which raises the bank of drawers and pigeonholes.

The year 1700 marks no great and sudden leap in the development of furniture, but if one takes the turn of the century to mark the middle of the period 1650-1750 and looks at what had been achieved between those two dates, the difference is immediately obvious. A gentleman of the 1650s would have been astonished by the quantity, quality, convenience and style of the furniture available by the 1750s.

The drastic change in style in fashionable European circles might well have been the most obvious difference, for the light and fantastic forms of the rococo had already been fully developed in France and they were quite unlike anything seen in the previous century. Indeed the 'modern' style developed during the first half of the 18th century and a definite reaction to the ponderous post-Renaissance forms which were the background to the formal life of the court of Louis XIV.

The extremes of curvaceous extravagance were only reached after a gradual relaxation of social conventions in France, especially during the Regency of the Duc d'Orléans from 1715 to 1723, when the court moved from Versailles to Paris, and during the early years of the reign of Louis XV himself, but the lightness and free form of a bureau plat or a commode of the mid-century would have seemed exotic indeed to 17th century eyes.

In Britain the rococo influence would have been evident, but less immediately so, for there it was competing with other exotic influences, like the Gothic and Chinese styles. This variety of stylistic influences might have hinted at an aspect of 18th century style: a much more rapid turn-over of fashionable forms. This trend was to become more noticeable during the following century, but the pace was increasing throughout the late 18th century.

Further removed from the centre of European fashion on the American continent, style would have seemed more conservative, based on English taste of a few years previously, but already developing distinctive characteristics like the bonnet tops on desks, bookcases and highboys.

In all parts of the Western world a mid-17th century observer would have been impressed by the quantity of furniture. The manufacture of high-quality pieces was no longer for the aristocracy only, and the 18th century furniture which remains a mainstay of the antiques trade is a physical reminder of just how much was produced.

Mid-18th century rooms do not seem to have been crammed with furniture in the way that Victorian parlours came to be. In fact, many contemporary illustrations of interiors show them to be a little bare by modern standards, and often quite formal, with pieces arranged around the wall. What is certain is that more people found themselves wealthy enough and felt secure enough to furnish their homes comfortably.

Increased comfort might have been the most alluring aspect of 18th century life. Good furniture had become not only more widespread, but also more diverse with specialized forms for specific purposes. Writing furniture, having been uncommon in the mid-17th century, was becoming normal in most homes a century later, and like everything else it was subject to specialization.

In 1650 most writing would have been done on a table, or at a simple table-top desk; by 1750 it was possible to choose from a range of established types of desk. In Britain the large bureau-cabinet with drawers beneath and paper storage above, was a standard piece by the mid-century. It was ideally suited to the day-to-day business of a household and it was adaptable.

Later in the century the upper part tended to be glazed, but the form of the typical English bureau meant that it could also be dispensed with all together without spoiling the appearance or usefulness of the desk.

Smaller versions with single doors in the upper part were popular for use in ladies' bedrooms or dressing rooms, although here a little kneehole dressing-table-cum-desk was also common.

In the library, itself a specialized room of growing importance in the 18th century, large pedestal desks that could be placed in the centre of a book-lined room were found most convenient.

In France the comfortable life had become something of a cult by the middle of the century. Louis XV set the example by building a whole suite of Petits Appartements at Versailles in which he could live in more relaxed fashion, away from the Grands Appartements created by his great grandfather Louis XIV.

The claustrophobic life of the stateroom and closet gave way to lifestyle closer to that of the well-off bourgeoisie and new and convenient pieces of furniture were made in the rococo style. The French court aspired to the elegant and informal disorder depicted in some of the paintings of Watteau, Boucher and Fragonard and the mood was gallant, light-hearted and relaxed compared to the previous century.

Much of the new furniture was very feminine. Upholstered chairs and sofas appeared alongside a clutter of little tables for sewing, reading and writing. Where a large desk was required the simple bureau plat was always popular in France and could be used in conjunction with a separate filing cabinet or cartonnier.

The French equivalent of the slope-front bureau, the bureau en pente, was still popular in 1750, but it was soon to be displaced by the sécrétaire à abattant and the secrétaire à cylindre.

In the very best writing furniture produced by the Paris ébénistes there is an attention to detail seldom found elsewhere. Creations such as the Bureau du Roi created for Louis XV by Oeben and finished by his successor Riesener combined elegance, convenience and ingenuity to a standard that was unmatched, even by the tour de force exhibition pieces seen in Europe a century later.

The cylinder front of the Bureau du Roi was in itself a technical innovation and the many mechanical surprises it embodies are a reminder that 18th century France was fascinated by science and technology, but such mechanical intricacy was expensive. The limited means of the middle classes in France, as in other countries, were stretched to more modest interpretations of the court style.

Perhaps the greatest contrast between 1650 and 1750 would have been experienced in the American colonies. Pioneer settlements had become thriving towns in many cases and elegant houses with gardens and carriage drives were beginning to appear. Here too elegant writing furniture in the form of slope-front desks and bookcases were part of the move towards a more comfortable life.

23. An English Queen Anne Walnut Bureau

This bureau is 3ft (91cm) wide, with a base of two long and two short drawers supported on bun feet. Walnut was the veneer selected by British cabinet-makers for most good-quality work until the 1730s. Timber from native trees was supplemented by imported European walnut, but the severe frosts of the winter of 1709 are said to have destroyed most of the walnut trees in Central Europe and by 1720 it had become so scarce that its export from France was banned. The problem was solved by the importation of black walnut from Virginia and by the almost universal adoption of mahogany as a veneer in the latter half of the century.

This bureau shows several signs of its pedigree. The heavy bun feet are a reminder of the late 17th century Dutch influence, whereas simple bracket feet were normal on most English bureaux by the mid-18th century. The bold dividing moulding around the centre of the body shows that this piece was conceived very much as a desk on a chest. The space from the level of the flap to the moulding (a well) could be used for storage: the opening was in the bottom of the writing compartment and closed by a lid.

24. An English Queen Anne Oak Bureau of *c*1710

This example is very compact at only 2ft (61cm) wide and equipped with a stepped interior and a well beneath the fall-front.

Honest oak pieces such as this continued to be made by country craftsmen to the traditional pattern right through the 18th century and beyond. Original handles and original feet are features to look out for on such pieces. Feet tended to wear out quickly with rough use and standing on damp floors; the tall brackets on this example are later replacements.

25. An English George I Walnut Bureau, *c*1715

This is a fairly early example of a standard English bureau of good quality.

It is veneered throughout with carefully-selected burr-wood, feather-and cross-banded, with two short and three long drawers graduated in size from top to bottom and cock-beaded around the edges. There is a fitted interior behind the fall front, which is supported on lopers when opened. The whole framework is supported on bracket feet and is 3ft 2in (96cm) wide.

Desks to this basic design continued to be made throughout the century.

23

24

25

26. An English Queen Anne Walnut Bureau Cabinet, early 18th century

Shown open and closed.

The double-domed mirror-glazed upper section contains 20 drawers of varying size, twelve of them with concave fronts, grouped around a central niche. The Corinthian pilasters have gilt capitals and bases and are partly stop-fluted. The arrangement of drawers in the base is fairly standard for the period, as are the mirror panels. The mirrors helped to magnify the light of candles placed on the slides which can be seen above the fall-front. This is a large desk, 3ft 3in (99cm) wide, and would have made an imposing fixture in any room, but the carrying handles suggest that it was considered portable.

27. An English Queen Anne Lacquered Bureau-Cabinet

This desk is 3ft 5¼in (1.04m) wide, decorated with a variety of chinoiserie scenes including large birds, figures in landscapes and flowering plants. The commanding double-domed cabinet is typical of early 18th-century English desks of this type, as are the arched mirrored panels on the doors. Other features which are commonly found at the beginning of the century but which die out later on are the candle slides beneath the mirrors, the ledge along the bottom edge of the fall-flap which allowed the slope to be used as a lectern for supporting books, and the deep space between the slope and the top drawers. Access to this space is via a lidded well in the bottom of the writing compartment. In later examples this space is more often occupied by further drawers.

Exotic japanned furniture remained popular in the early part of the century, having been introduced from Holland after the Restoration and explained to English craftsmen in Stalker and Parker's *Treatise of Japanning and Varnishing* of 1688, which included 'Patterns for Japan-work in imitation of the Indians for Tables, Stands, Frames, Cabinets etc.' Japanning also seems to have been considered a suitable occupation for the amateur artist.

26

27

28

29

28. An English Red-Japanned Bureau-Cabinet, early 18th century

Supported on gilt hairy paw feet; the bureau has a base of two short and two long drawers, and a writing compartment over a storage well.

This is a fine example of the most extrovert of all 18th-century English furniture forms, markedly different from the staid mahogany bureau-bookcases which became the standard Georgian product later in the century. This bureau is unusual in that the mirrored outer doors, when opened as here, reveal three glazed panels, the central one hinged as a door. The cabinet behind the panels is unfitted but splendidly decorated; the brilliance of the gilt butterflies, and grape clusters on their bright red ground is a reminder of the original effect of the whole before light and dirt dimmed the exterior. The width of this piece is 3ft 1in (94cm).

29. An English Queen Anne Red Lacquer Escritoire

The fanciful chinoiserie scenes in gold are a spectacular form of ornament which is relatively common on bureau bookcases of the period but rare on escritoires. There are two short and two long drawers in the base, a long concealed drawer in the cushion cornice at the top, and a variety of small drawers and pigeonholes around a cupboard in the upper section. The fall-front is fitted with a rising velvet-lined writing slope. It is 3ft 7in (1.09m) wide.

30. An English George I Walnut-Veneered Chest

Chests of this kind, in which the top folds out to form a table or desk supported on lopers like those found on English bureaux, were made throughout the first half of the 18th century and are usually referred to as "bachelor's chests", which may be a contemporary term. The design provided storage and a place to sit for those with limited space.

This piece is 2ft 8in (81cm) wide, with a heavy hinged top.

31. An English George I Walnut Kneehole Desk, *c*1720

An unusual feature of this desk is the fitted writing compartment behind a fall-front. It also has a folding top. The lower section, with three drawers in each pedestal and a cupboard at the back of the kneehole, is the normal pattern for desks of this type, but it is rare to find an 18th-century English piece with a lockable writing compartment of this kind. The width of this desk if 3ft 1½in (95cm).

32. An English George I Walnut Kneehole Bureau

Beneath the flap, which is decoratively quarter-veneered and baize-lined, the writing compartment is fitted with a cupboard, four drawers and pigeonholes. This early 18th-century piece, perhaps intended for a lady's bedroom, clearly shows its ancestry, being a simple combination of the commoner kneehole desk and the slope-front table desk, divided all round by a moulding. This example is 2ft 5in (74.5cm) wide, and has six small drawers flanking another drawer over a cupboard in the kneehole. Such pieces often doubled as dressing tables; some are fitted for that purpose.

33. An English Portable Table Desk, *c*1730

Shown open and closed.

Under the flap are five drawers and three pigeonholes, and the single base drawer has a shaped block front cut from solid beech. The main carcase is of pine, red japanned and decorated with chinoiseries in gold and silver. It is 1ft 3½in (39cm) wide.

33a. An English Walnut-Veneered Table Bureau, *c*1705

The diamond-and-leaf-inlaid fall-front opens to give access to a fitted interior and forms a writing surface supported on a pair of tiny lopers with ring handles. Similar ring handles are fitted to the chevron-banded drawer below. This desk is a slightly more sophisticated reminder of the simple slope-topped boxes of the previous century.

30

33a

32

33

31

34. An American William and Mary Slope-Front Desk, *c*1720–30

This desk was made in Pennsylvania, and is walnut-veneered with two short and two long drawers in the base. It is 2ft 9¾in (86cm) wide.

With its one-piece design and shaped, stepped interior of small drawers and pigeonholes around a central cupboard, this desk has all the basic characteristics of the typical piece of writing furniture of the 18th century. Tell-tale early features are the turned ball-and-cone feet and the brass pear-drop handles.

35. An American William and Mary Slant-Front Desk, *c*1710–1725

The carcase, 2ft 10in (86cm) wide, is of pine and maple, with a simple open compartment beneath the slope and two drawers in the frieze. The whole desk rests on a joined stand, with turned legs and is mortice and tenoned together.

36. A French Régence Period Bureau Plat, *c*1720

Veneered in kingwood and mounted with gilt bronze espagnolettes, masks, foliate scrolls and leafy handles, this 6ft 7in (2m) wide desk is a good example of the so-called Régence style, which represented a gradual transition from the massive and formal baroque of Louis XIV's reign to the light and fanciful rococo of Louis XV's mid-reign. Three drawers are fitted into the frieze along one side, but those on the other side are dummy drawers.

37. A French Louis XV Bureau Plat, *c*1730

This desk was made by Charles Cressent, who was *ébéniste* to Philippe, Duc d'Orléans, regent for Louis XV until 1723. (He was also an accomplished sculptor and was taken to court and fined on several occasions for modelling, casting and gilding his own mounts, which, under guild regulations, was explicitly the province of the *fondeurs* and *doreurs*.) As the leading *ébéniste* of the Régence period, Cressent presided over the gradual lightening of the more formal Louis XIV style which was a feature of the early years of the 18th century. This bureau retains a certain stately quality, not least because of its width being 6ft 9in (2.05m), but this is countered by the characteristic rococo C-scrolls of the drawer handles, with their sprigs of wayward leaves, and by the sweep of the central escutcheon. It has a leather-lined top with three drawers in the shaped frieze and is mounted with finely-modelled caryatids at the angles and bearded masks flanking the central drawer.

34

35

36

37

38. An American Queen Anne Blockfront Mahogany Kneehole Desk, c1730–40

There are three drawers on each side of the kneehole cupboard and one long drawer across the top, giving an overall width of 2ft 8in (81cm). The delicate stringing and multi-coloured star inlay (four-pointed on the cupboard door, twelve-pointed on the top) is of a type found on many American Queen Anne pieces and was probably copied from London cabinetmakers. This example was made in Massachusetts.

During the American Chippendale period carving became the dominant form of decoration, but contrasted veneers were used a great deal during the Federal period.

39. An American Queen Anne Walnut Kneehole Desk, c1745

Made at Newport, Rhode Island, it has a width of 2ft 9½in (85cm). Supported on bracket feet, the desk has one long frieze drawer, small deep drawers down each pedestal and a panelled cupboard in the back of the kneehole.

40. An American Queen Anne Mahogany Desk-and-Bookcase, c1735–1750

From Boston, Massachusetts, this double-domed desk is 3ft 4½in (1.03m) wide, and is in two parts, with carrying handles on the sides of the top and bottom sections. It has a four-drawer base beneath a fitted interior with small drawers, pigeonholes and document drawers behind the two pilasters with flame finials. In the centre is a cupboard, often called a prospect drawer in America. The shelved upper section is unusual in that it has gold-painted shells decorating the alcoves behind the arched mirror-panelled doors. One of the candleslides is shown in use here to demonstrate how the mirrors helped to reflect light back into the room.

41. An American Queen Anne Maple Desk-and-Bookcase, c1740

There are compartmented shelves and pigeonholes behind the panelled doors in the upper section and a stepped fitted interior without a central cupboard. This is a good example of the plainer style of Rhode Island cabinet-work, without any of the shell carving or blockfronts usually associated with the more famous Newport craftsmen. It is 3ft (91cm) wide.

42. An American Walnut Desk-and-Cabinet, c1745–50

This early example of block-and-shell carving from Newport, Rhode Island, is 3ft (91cm) wide.

The panels of the cabinet doors are raised and headed with convex carved shells, while concave shell carving is used to enrich the block-front interior of the desk. The base has a plain, straight front of graduated drawers resting on ogee feet.

43. An American Queen Anne Black Walnut Desk on Frame

This is a fairly sophisticated version of the rudimentary slope-front desk mounted on a lowboy, which was to be found in the American colonies from the beginning of the 18th century. This example is 3ft 2½in (98cm) wide and was made in Philadelphia c1750. Here the lowboy has the usual arrangement of two small and one long drawer, while the desk is stylishly fitted with little serpentine drawers and pigeonholes to either side of a cupboard containing four more drawers. The drawers are all fitted with spurs to prevent them being pulled out inadvertently. The simple scalloped apron on the base is a traditional form of decoration, but the cabiole legs with ball-and-claw feet and the quarter-columns in both desk and base reflect the growing sophistication of the late Queen Anne period in America.

42

43

40

38

39

41

44. A French Louis XV Rosewood Veneered Bureau Plat, c1750

This large and handsome desk is traditionally supposed to have belonged to the Compte de Vergennes, Louis XVI's Foreign Minister. Certainly the bureau was amongst the furniture in the *Ministère des Affaires Etrangères* in 1901 when it was moved to the Louvre for public display. It was made by Pierre II Migeon and Jacques Dubois and has gilt bronze leafy mounts, three frieze drawers and a shaped leather-lined writing surface which is 6ft 6in (1.99mm) wide.

45. A French Louis XV Bureau Plat

This tulipwood and kingwood desk was made by Bernard II van Risenburgh. It is 6ft (1.83m) wide. Below the shaped serpentine top, the three frieze drawers are balanced by three dummy drawers on the opposite side. The marquetry flowersprays which decorate the featherbanded kingwood drawer fronts and the sides of the desk are typical of van Risenburgh, who was one of the most accomplished *ébénistes* of the Louis XV period. He was known only by his abbreviated *estampille* of BVRB until the late 1950s, when his full name and identity were finally discovered.

46. A French late Louis XV Green *Vernis Martin* Bureau Plat

This desk has a matching *cartonnier* and inkstand, and all were made by René Dubois, *maître* in 1754. The bureau is 4ft 8½in (1.43m) wide, the *cartonnier* 6ft 10in (2.08m) high. Bureaux plats were often made with matching *cartonniers* or filing cabinets. Some are no more than small *gradins*, designed to stand at one end of a large desk, but this magnificent example is free-standing. Here it has been turned at an angle to show the gilt decoration of martial trophies on the bottom panels, but it was intended to stand at one end of the desk within easy reach of the writer and the cupboard doors are on each side rather than the front. There are also small drawers in the frieze at each side, while the top section is divided into three velvet-lined compartments. The details of the ornament are all gilt, crowned by the embracing figures of Cupid and Psyche on a spirally-fluted drum with Peace and War to either side. The trophies on the doors in the base represent Learning and Agriculture.

45

48

44

46

49

47

47. A French Louis XV Secrétaire à Abattant

The secrétaire à abattant first came into fashion as a large piece of case furniture in the 1750s, but examples in rococo style like this one are far less common than those of a few years later in the more formal neo-classical style. This tulipwood-veneered example, does, however, show all the features of the more typical Louis XVI secrétaires. The large shaped flat in the upper section folds down to give access to six small drawers and pigeonholes decorated with sprays of flowers tied with ribbons to echo the exterior end-cut marquetry, and there is a two-door cupboard in the base. Just beneath the serpentine marble top, nearly 5ft (1.50m) from the floor, there is a shaped drawer in the frieze. It was made by Christophe Wolff, who became *maître* in 1755.

48. A French Mid-18th Century Kingwood Secrétaire à Abattant

Pieces like this one, which show the rounded, rococo characteristics of the Louis XV period combined with the sterner lines of the Louis XVI period, are often referred to as being in Transitional style, a term which emphasises the gradual way in which French furniture styles tended to evolve in the 18th century. This example has a brown marble top veined with white above a fall-front with rounded corners which conceals an interior of shelves and four drawers, one of which is fitted with an inkwell and a pounce pot. The doors below hide more shelves and a *coffre fort* (strong box). It was made by Jean Demoulin, maître in 1749, and is 2ft 8in (81cm) wide.

49. A Small French Late Louis XV Secrétaire à Abattant

This piece is 3ft 2in (97cm) wide, veneered in a variety of woods, mounted with gilt-bronze lion heads and masks, garlands and swags and with plaques of flower-painted Sèvres porcelain. It is probably from the workshop of Martin Carlin, who specialized in porcelain-mounted pieces. Small secretaires like this one, in the form of *meubles d'entre deux* (a cupboard with curved shelves on each side), enjoyed a period of popularity in France in the third quarter of the 18th century and they were later copied by English makers. Sheraton illustrates one, described as a lady's cabinet in his *Cabinet-Maker and Upholsterer's Drawing-Book* (Plate XVI).

50. A French Louis XV Kingwood-Veneered Secrétaire-en-Pente

This piece, 4ft 6¾in (1.39m) wide, was built in two stages with two drawers over two cupboards in the base and a stepped interior of pigeonholes and drawers (one fitted for writing materials) behind a fall front which is supported on steel rods with brass knobs pulled out of the body. This is a high-quality piece with fine rococo mounts of gilt bronze, but its rather awkward two-part design, at variance with the sinuous curves of the applied decoration, suggests that this may be a very early example of the secrétaire-en-pente, which was only introduced to France in the 1730s. Like many early English examples it is fitted with a storage well with a sliding lid in the bottom of the writing compartment.

51. A large French Louis XV Tulipwood Parquetry Bureau en Pente

Stamped for Pierre Migeon (1701–1758), this desk is of the *galbé* (curved) form typical of French rococo slope-front desks, but is unusual for its size (5ft 1in (1.55m) wide) and for the arrangement of the drawers – there are two above the kneehole and three more on the lefthand side, but those on the right are dummies, with the three true drawers opening out of the side of the base. The flap itself is divided into two parts and encloses a *coffre fort* (strong box) along with three small drawers and shelves. The flat surface above the stepped top may have been intended to take a filing box or some other accessory.

52. A French Kingwood and Marquetry Bureau en Pente

3ft 9in (1.14m) wide, this desk of sinuous serpentine form with one long and two short drawers in the base, shows decoration which is typical of the *ébéniste*. The bombé sloping lid is inlaid, like the rest of the desk, with flower sprays on quartered grounds. It is stamped RVLC, the mark of Roger Vandercruse, who was also known as Lacroix, and tended to specialize in delicate marquetry work. He became *maître* in 1755, and died in 1799.

53. A French Louis XV Period Bonheur-du-Jour

Nearly all the surfaces of this desk are decorated with a marquetry of tulipwood, pear, satinwood and others, in imitation of oriental lacquer subjects. The central landscape panel is flanked by flower vases on the doors of the cupboards and there is a more extensive still life on the undertier, which is shaped at the front to make it easier to sit at the desk when it is in use. There are two cupboards and a drawer in the upper section and a single drawer in the frieze. The width of this desk is 2ft 7in (79cm).

54. A French Louis XV Bonheur-du-Jour

This is the work of Jean-Baptiste Vassou, who became a *maître ébéniste* in 1767. It is 2ft 11in (63cm) wide and made of tulipwood and amaranth decorated with trellis marquetry interspersed with flower sprays. The pierced superstructure has three small drawers across the bottom and the writing surface is lined with leather. The frieze drawer contains a series of compartments with flaps.

55. A French Louis XV Black-Lacquered Bonheur-du-Jour, *c*1766

This 2ft 2½in (67cm) wide desk is mounted with gilt bronze and with 17 shaped panels of Sèvres soft-paste porcelain painted with bouquets of flowers. The three-drawer *gradin* with three-quarter gallery is fixed to the body by dowels. The single frieze drawer is fitted with a writing surface that hinges back to reveal a storage compartment and a narrow compartment on the right for writing materials. This is one of about ten similar bonheurs-du-jour by the German-born Paris *ébéniste* Martin Carlin which can be dated by the marks on the porcelain to the 1760s. They are thought to have been commissioned by the influential *marchands-merciers* Simon-Philippe Poirier and Dominique Daguerre, who also bought various other small stands, desks and work tables with Sèvres plaques from Carlin.

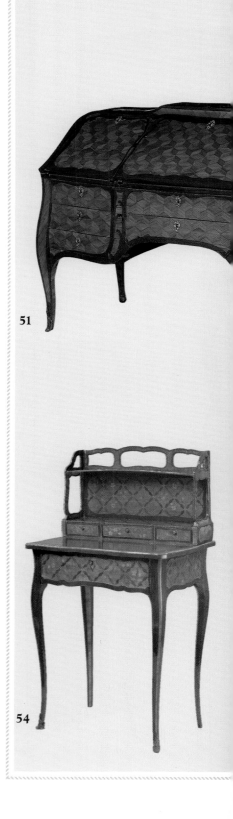

51

54

52

55

53

50

56. A French Louis XV Period Table à Écrire

The understated asymmetry and delicate rocaille work are only echoes of the high rococo style. It has restrained rococo ormolu mounts and is veneered in kingwood with a shaped quartered top (2ft 5¾in (76cm) wide) and diagonally banded legs and frieze. The leather-lined writing slide is pulled out by means of a little ormolu knob and the drawer in the end is fitted with silvered inkwells and a pen tray.

57. A French Louis XV Petite Table à Écrire

This kind of desk seems to have been an important piece of furniture for French ladies in the middle of the 18th century. Like many of these tables, it does not reveal its intended use until the frieze drawer is opened to show a leather-lined flap and fittings for writing below the sliding top, which is 2ft 1¼in (64cm) wide. The end-cut marquetry decoration of flowers and leaves and the bold tulipwood veneer of the cabriole legs are the work of Léonard Boudin, who became *maître* in 1761. His *estampille*, "L BOUDIN JME" is struck on the carcase twice over.

58. A French Louis XV Tulipwood and Kingwood Table à Écrire

With its delicate cabriole legs and ormolu mounts, this piece is typical of the many little portable tables found in 18th-century French interiors. It is 2ft 1½in (64.5cm) wide, with a serpentine tray top inlaid with a marquetry flower spray within a kidney-shaped border. A leather-lined slide pulls out over two drawers, one of which is fitted for writing equipment.

57

59

59. A French Louis XV Tulipwood and Purplewood Table à Écrire

The lobed top, marquetry-decorated with flowers within a scrolling leafy border, is 2ft 4in (71cm) wide. The frieze drawer in the front is fitted with a writing slope with hinged, lidded compartments on either side decorated to match the top and containing little drawers. There are also small drawers at either end of the desk. The fabric firescreen at the back is supported by an extending pantograph of steel rods. The ormolu mounts at the angles are a good example of rococo rocaille work.

60. A French Louis XV Kingwood Table à Écrire

The lobed cube-parquetry top, 2ft 8¾in (83cm) wide, incorporates a leather-lined bookrest on a rachet and a pull-up firescreen. The screen, intended to shield delicate complexions from the heat of the open fire, folds down into the desk when not in use and the fillet which forms its upper frame fits neatly into the top. In the front there is a slide which pulls out for writing and there are drawers at each end. This is the work of Pierre Migeon II, one of the principal *ébénistes* of his time (*maître c*1738). He has relied for most of his decorative effect on the crossbanding and feather banding of the rich grain of the kingwood. The only ormolu feature on the cabriole legs are small shell-cast angles or *chutes* and matching toes or *sabots*.

61. A French Louis XV Kingwood Parquetry Secrétaire-de-Voyage

In this picture it is shown open to reveal a few of its many secret drawers. The block of drawers on the right normally forms the interior of the double-doored cabinet in the base, but a secret catch allows it to be removed to reveal many more drawers with leather tab handles on the inside. The central drawer of the removable section is here taken out to show the further drawer which normally lies behind it. There are yet more little drawers in the well in the floor of the writing compartment, a long drawer in the side of the desk just above the carrying handle and a further slide below the fall. It is quite small (1ft 4in (41cm) wide), but every space has been put to use.

62. A French Secrétaire à la Bourgogne

This is a form of mechanical writing table that was in vogue in Paris in the 1760s. Though only 2ft 8in (81cm) wide, it is packed with displays of technical virtuosity and decorated with no fewer than 24 marquetry panels, covering almost every surface, including those normally hidden in the body of the table.

The top is inlaid with a picture of a classical ruin and one of the pieces of fallen masonry conceals a lock which releases the front half of the top. This folds forward to form a writing surface with a leather lining.

The whole of the back half of the top rises at the touch of a button to reveal a bank of small drawers and a central niche with a tambour front. All the drawers are themselves opened by spring catches, and a catch behind the tambour releases a collapsible bookrest which can be pulled out and used as required.

More surprises spring from the body of the front half of the desk, with a central nest of six small drawers flanked by hinged lidded compartments.

This desk is unmarked but similarly complex examples are known to have been made by Jean-François Oeben and other German cabinetmakers working in Paris who were known for their mechanical expertise.

63. A French Mid-18th-Century Secrétaire à Culbute

The cherrywood this piece is made of is inlaid with geometric lines and a central Maltese cross in amaranth. This fairly humble piece, 2ft 1in (64cm) wide, is a rare survival of an interesting form of folding desk which proved more ingenious than practical. The hinged top is adjustable, allowing the desk to be multi-functional: as shown here, with the lid closed, it is a small side table. For reading, the top can be lifted to the angle desired and held by single strut, while a small section in the middle of the front can be hinged upwards to form a convenient rest for the book. The top can also be hinged open completely to form a leather-lined writing surface (see detail). The sloping box underneath can then be lifted upwards from the well of the desk to reveal itself as a fitted compartment with drawers and shelves for storing writing accessories. In practice the hinged mechanism proved fragile and the drawer section was heavy and inconvenient to lift into position. This desk seems to have originally been fitted with a sliding fire screen at the back and candleholders in the brass sockets at the tops of the front legs.

64. A detail of the Secrétaire à Culbute, viewed from above, with the leather-lined flap folded forward and the hinged compartment ready to be lifted into position. Note the strut on the right for adjusting the slope of the top when in use as a bookrest.

65. A Louis XV Rosewood, Tulipwood and Satinwood Meuble à Écrire Debout

This was made by the Paris *ébéniste* Joseph Baumhauer for Count Karl of Cobentzl, a minister for Empress Maria Theresa in the Austrian Netherlands. Baumhauer received a royal warrant *c*1755.

It is a most unusual piece and was made to a very high standard, with particular attention paid to the matching of the ormolu framing and the cabinetwork. The main body has an interior of shelves, veneered throughout with rosewood. The concealed drawers at each side have fronts disguised as part of the ormolu framing of the marquetry panels. On the top is a fixed leather-lined slope with a small drawer in the side. It is 3ft 5in (1.05m) wide and 3ft 10in (1.18m) high, so that a person can stand at it and write. This desk is a typical example of the way in which much Paris furniture of the time was supplied to foreign patrons. It was sold on 9 August 1758 by the *marchand-mercier* Lazare Duvaux to M. de Meulan, who was the Count's agent. He then dispatched the cabinet to the Count in Brussels.

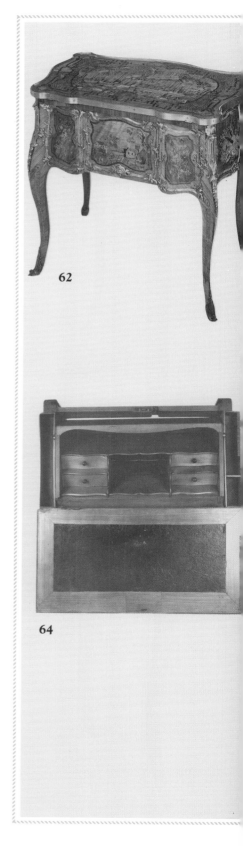

62

64

63

65

61

66. The Bureau du Roi Louis XV

This elaborate bureau à cylindre, perhaps the first ever made, took nine years to complete. It was begun by Jean François Oeben in 1760, and when Oeben died in 1763 the work was carried on by his successor in business, Jean Henri Riesener. The bureau is signed in marquetry at the back *Riesener H. 1769 à l'Arsenal de Paris*. It was designed for the study or *cabinet intérieur* of Louis XV, where it stood until the Revolution.

The exterior, dominated by magnificent gilt-bronze mounts, is decorated with fine marquetry panels. The roll-top itself is decorated with three cartouches representing Learning and the Arts flanked by Dramatic and Lyric Poetry. The frieze and the double drawers on each side of the kneehole are decorated with ribbon-tied flower sprays, as are the corresponding panels on the sides and the back. The upper side panels are decorated with military trophies, and at the back there is a central gilt-bronze plaque depicting putti holding up a portrait medallion of Minerva, flanked by marquetry panels emblematic of Mathematics and Astronomy. Documentary evidence suggests that the blue and white *biscuit de Sèvres* plaques of the Three Graces on the lower side panels replace royal ciphers which were defaced during the French Revolution. The clock in the centre of the gallery is double-sided.

Oeben, in common with many Paris-based German craftsmen, was renowned for his use of mechanical devices to release hidden drawers and convert furniture to other uses. In this desk the tambour slide opens at the touch of a button to reveal small drawers flanking a pigeonhole and a writing surface divided into three leather-lined panels. The centre panel is raised by a button to form a reading stand, and beneath it is a well containing three drawers. There is also a secret drawer on the lefthand side of the interior.

The desk, for many years on view at the Louvre in Paris and now back at Versailles, was much admired during the 19th century and several replicas were made to a very high standard.

Details of lion pelt mounts from the three desks

The hanging lions' pelts used as mounts above the knees of the legs on all three desk. The original from the Bureau du Roi (a) was meticulously copied and finished for the 1786 bureau plat (b), but the 1880s version (c) is a mere pastiche with a rat-like tail.

67. A Bureau Plat

This 6ft 2½in (1.90m) wide desk was made for the *Cabinet Intérieur* at Versailles as a companion piece to the Bureau du Roi and delivered in December 1786. This bureau echoes the cylinder desk very faithfully, particularly in the meticulous copying of the mounts. Both desks were already out of vogue when they were made, but harmony of style was obviously considered more important than high fashion. The central drawer of the bureau plat does, however, tend more towards the restrained neo-classical taste of the 1780s in the simple rectangular beaded border around the marquetry panel. The drawer also projects slightly from the desk, whereas the one on the original is slightly inset. The decoration of the end panels of the bureau plat is worth noting. Gilt-bronze cornucopiae pour forth an abundance of marquetry fruit as on the Bureau du Roi, but the central medallions are inlaid with interlaced *LL* monogram. Evidently the monogram was made to match the ones later removed from the Bureau du Roi and replaced by porcelain plaques.

The bureau plat is well documented and the original costing of the job is recorded. Of the overall cost of 5716 livres, 25% went to Guillaume Beneman, the German cabinetmaker who replaced Riesener as court *ébéniste* in 1785, for the cabinetwork; 11% went on the marquetry, but by far the largest amount, 58%, was spent on the mounts, particularly the chasing and gilding. Making wax models of the original, locks and packing made up the other 6%. After the Revolution the bureau plat was sold at one of the many auctions of royal furniture for 5000 livres – less than cost price.

68. A Detail of the Back of the 19th-Century Copy showing the central gilt-bronzed plaque with seven putti grouped around a portrait medallion of Minerva.

69. A Bureau à Cylindre, *c*1880

This was inspired the Bureau du Roi but differs in several important respects. The flamboyant mounts on the top part of the original desk – the twin-branch candelabra supporting a youth and a nymph, the clock with reclining putti, the urn finials – have here been omitted entirely, without spoiling the overall balance of the piece, and the slatted tambour of the 18th-century desk has been replaced by a solid cylinder which is more robust and less likely to jam. The overall shape and the ormulu mounts on the base of the desk are closely based on the original, although the lion pelt castings at the corners are noticeably less fine. Some of the marquetry panels also differ.

67

68

66

69

70. A Venetian *Lacca Povera* Bureau-Cabinet of the Mid-18th Century

It stands 8ft 7½in (2.63m) to the top of the cartouche. The mitre and cross-key cresting on the cartouche suggests that the original owner may have been a pope. The four figures have not been identified. It has a simply fitted writing compartment behind the fall-front, with cupboards, recesses and drawers in the two-door cabinet and a serpentine-fronted chest of drawers as a base, but its most striking feature is the landscape and figure decoration in brown, green and yellow on a bright red ground with gilt enrichments.

Venetian craftsmen specialized in producing highly-decorative pieces, and the theatrical effect was often heightened by the use of the *lacca povera* or *lacca contrafatta* technique, whereby prints were cut out and stuck to the surface before being varnished. This differed from other European imitations of Oriental lacquer in which the relief decoration was built up layer by layer.

71. A North Italian Walnut Bureau, 1730

The overall delicate inlay is of engraved bone. The main decorative motifs are flowerheads, joined by scrolling tendrils and interspersed with grotesque masks, strange winged beasts and other intriguing devices, including a pair of duelling dwarves at the centre of the shaped fall-front. Beneath the flap is a writing compartment fitted with drawers, and the main body, 3ft 9in (1.14m) wide, is fitted with long drawers shaped in the distinctive manner of South German and North Italian makers of the period.

70

71

72

73

72. A German Walnut Bureau-Cabinet

This 4ft 2in (1.27m)-wide piece was probably made in Wurzburg or Mainz c1740. It is made in two parts. The serpentine-fronted top section has a two-door cupboard, four small drawers down each of the shaped sides, and a narrow drawer in the pediment. There are two more small drawers in the sloped sections on either side of the slope-front writing compartment, and three long drawers in the ox-bow-fronted base. The rococo had a strong influence on German craftsmen and this fine-quality piece is embellished with carved rocaille work and scrolls and inlaid throughout with strapwork and asymmetrical motifs in walnut, pear and ebony. The sloping sections on either side of the fall and the multiplicity of small drawers are typical features of German writing furniture of the mid-18th century.

73. A Mid-18th Century South German Walnut Bureau

The strapwork veneer and other parquetry motifs decorate a ground of crossbanding and panels of burr walnut. The exaggerated shape of the three base drawers, canted outwards at the sides and echoed by the small drawers in the upper section, is a distinctive feature of this type of desk. The width is 4ft 2½in (1.28m).

74. A Danish Painted Bureau-Cabinet, Early 18th Century

It is 4ft 5in (1.35m) wide, decorated with figures, landscapes and buildings, and with borders imitating oriental lacquer and grounds of imitation red marble. It has a remarkably shallow fall front concealing a fitted interior, and an upper cabinet of drawers and pigeonholes behind double doors.

75. A Dutch Marquetry Bureau-Cabinet of the Mid-18th Century

Bureaux of this kind, with scrolling flower decoration, canted corners with characteristic bombé projections, and usually with stepped and shaped cornices and bold claw feet, were made in large quantities in Holland in the 18th century. Many copies were also made in the 19th century.

This one is 4ft 2½in (1.28m) wide, with a two-door display cabinet in the upper part and a writing compartment beneath a serpentine fall-front in the lower part. There are three drawers in the base and cupboards in the angles on each side.

76. An Early 18th Century German Rarity

This bureau cabinet of c1730, 3ft 1in (94cm) wide, is of fairly conventional form with a fall-front writing compartment containing three small drawers beneath a cupboard flanked by more small drawers over candleslides and a base of three drawers, but it is highly unusual in being veneered throughout in alabaster. Examples of Italian furniture veneered in stone are known, but it is rare to find it from any other source. This example is embellished with shaped carved panels and with finely worked terms at each of the four corners of the base.

77. A Mid-18th-Century German Oak Bureau-Cabinet

This curious piece is of imposing size, 7ft 9in (2.36m) wide and 7ft 6in (2.30m) high to the top of the rococo cartouche containing a gilt monogram. There are cupboards above and below the slope-front writing compartment, but they are out-numbered by no fewer than 49 drawers of various shapes and sizes. Small shaped-front drawers are a feature of German rococo bureaux, but it is unusual to find quite so many of them in a single piece.

74

75

76

77

78. An English George II Mahogany Bureau-on-Stand of the Mid-18th Century

Bureaux of this design continued to be made up until the middle of the 18th century, but they are not nearly so common as the conventional type developed from a desk and a chest of drawers. Here the two-part origin can be clearly seen, with a fitted writing compartment behind the fall-front over a single drawer as the upper section, and a single-drawer unit as the stand. The fashion for the classic combination of cabriole leg with ball-and-claw foot (here carved at the knees with acanthus leaf decoration), had passed its peak by the mid-18th century in England, but it continued to be almost standard on good-quality furniture for much longer in America. It is quite small at 2ft 4in (71cm) wide.

79. An English Mahogany Bureau Bookcase, c1742

This fine quality bureau was made by the London cabinetmaker John Channon for a Bristol merchant, Henry Hobhouse, and is 4ft 3in (1.92m) wide.

The use of gilding, the shaped surrounds of the mirror panels and the architectural design with a broken, dentil-decorated pediment supported on fluted Corinthian pilasters are typical London features of the period. The fine brass inlay on the fall-front, which incorporates a concealed keyhole in the centre, is a Channon speciality. The interior of the writing compartment is beautifully fitted. (*See detail.*)

80. A detail of the fine fitted interior of the Channon bureau.

Note how the architectural design of the exterior is echoed in a central mirrored cupboard with steps leading up to it. Many bureaux are fitted with concealed compartments, but in this example almost every component in the interior slides out to reveal a hiding place. The steps and the pilasters on either side of the door, the fluted pilasters between the drawers and the shaped section on the extreme right are all secret compartments. Even the divisions between the pigeonholes slide forward to disclose hidden spaces.

81. An English Mahogany Bureau-Bookcase, c1760

This 3ft 8in (1.12m) wide desk has a typical arrangement of four long drawers beneath a slope-front. The standard thirteen-pane glazing pattern has been enriched by the inclusion of four gothic-inspired motifs and the gothic theme is echoed by the arched tracery at the centre of a pierced fretwork design beneath the swan-neck pediment.

82. An English George III Mahogany Bureau-Bookcase, c1765

This is a typical piece of the period. Glass-fronted bookcases in combination with a bureau base became firm favourites in the second half of the century. The panes, fixed in a tracery of wooden glazing bars, were arranged in a great variety of ways, but this thirteen-pane pattern was a standard. The glazing bars are often referred to as astragals because they were made of semi-circular mouldings of that name.

79

80

82

78

81

83. An English George III Mahogany Secretaire-Bookcase

This desk is 3ft 7in (1.09m) wide, with an arcaded cornice and a frieze of imitation fluting above a glazed bookcase and a serpentine-fronted base of three long drawers and a secretaire. The top two drawer-fronts are dummies forming the fall-flap of the writing compartment. The slight curving of the base, combined with a careful selection of veneer which allows the figure to continue over the whole surface, mark this out as a piece of some quality. The upper doors, each formed from eleven panes separated by glazing bars in the form of urns, are unusual and enterprising if a little clumsy in their final effect. Intricate glazing patterns were a feature of English bookcase desks after the glass front became popular in the second half of the 18th century. Diamond and lanceolate tracery patterns were favoured, often giving a slight Chinese or Gothic taste to a piece of otherwise conventional design.

84. A Mid-18th century English Mahogany Breakfront Secretaire-Bookcase

With its pagoda roof and intricate chinoiserie tracery on the bookcase doors, this is an extreme example of the Chinese style popularized by Chippendale's *Director* in the 1750s. Few makers attempted so thorough a pastiche of Chinese architecture. 6ft 2in (1.88m) wide, this desk has a fitted writing drawer over a double cupboard in the centre and six short drawers down each side.

83

84

85

86

85. An English George III Mahogany Secretaire-Cabinet

This unusual piece appears to be loosely based on a plate in the third (1762) edition of Chippendale's *Director*, which is described as 'A Lady's Writing Table and Bookcase'. The writing surface is a slide over compartments in the central frieze drawer. The upper section has shelves in the shaped flanking cupboards and there are small drawers, pigeonholes and a cupboard behind the central door. The top five drawers are fitted with silver plates marked *Bills Paid, Bills Not Paid, Receipts, Letters Answered* and *Letters Not Answered;* the little cupboard below conceals an iron safe. In stylistic terms this is a rare English example of a cabinet dating from the transitional period of the 1760s. The shaped top and pierced pediment and gallery look back to the rococo, but the anthemion finial and fluted tapering legs are neo-classical. It is 3ft 7in (1.09m) wide.

86. An English George III Mahogany Secretaire-Chest

The open superstructure of this desk is Chinese fretwork of the type popularised by Chippendale's *Director*, topped by four urn finials of turned ivory. The base has a secretaire drawer over two short and three long graduated drawers. Tall, narrow chests of this kind (it measures 2ft 6in (76cm) across), in which the two top drawers are dummies disguising fitted writing compartments, were the height of elegant design in the 1760s.

87. An English George II Walnut Library Desk, c 1740

This is a small example of its kind, 4ft (1.22m) wide, with a leather inset top, cupboards on either side of the kneehole, one of which contains drawers, and a shallow drawer at each end of the frieze. The monumental treatment of this piece, with its scrolling monopodia topped by lion masks and terminating in claw feet, is typical of a lot of the furniture produced in England during the second quarter of the 18th century. The Palladian style, based on the work of the Italian architect Andrea Palladio (1508–80) had a second flowering during this period under the influence of the English architect William Kent, having first influenced British design in the early 17th century when it was introduced by Inigo Jones (1573–1652). The heavy, classically-inspired forms were very different from the dainty rococo experiments that were at the forefront of French design at the same time.

88. An English Mahogany Library Writing Table, c1758

This desk is characteristic of the mid-18th century Gothic Revival. It is now at Temple Newsam House, Leeds, but it was made for the Countess of Pomfret's house, Pomfret Castle in Arlington Street, apparently the only Gothic Revival house in central London (now demolished). The desk is 6ft 8in (2.03m) wide, with a leather-inset top supported on four pedestals decorated with medallions of applied Gothic tracery and with engaged cluster columns at the corners. There are three shallow drawers in the frieze down each of the long sides and each pedestal contains three drawers behind a door of solid mahogany. Most of the rest of the desk is of mahogany veneer on a pine carcase. The Gothic Revival affected the decoration of various types of furniture, but it was particularly well suited to library furniture; tall shelving and large, imposing desks like this one lent themselves to an architectural treatment.

89. An English Mahogany Library Desk, c1750

In Chippendale rococo style, this desk has a 5ft-(1.52m)-wide leather-lined top supported on serpentine-fronted pedestals with carved scrolling pilasters at the canted corners. The drawers, which are all fitted with brass handles in rococo style, are arranged in an interesting manner: each pedestal contains three drawers in one side and a cupboard in the other, but all the drawers in the frieze on the long sides are dummies. Each end, however, is fitted with a working drawer in the frieze, one of them fitted with an adjustable writing slope and a pair of retractable circular candle stands. This fine desk, which is very close to designs in Chippendale's *Director*, is a good example of the generally muted English approach to the rococo or 'French' style.

90. A Mid-18th-Century English Mahogany Kneehole Desk

2ft 6in (76cm) wide, this desk has a long frieze drawer and three small drawers in each pedestal. The shallow cupboard in the back of the kneehole is a distinctive feature of these desks, which were particularly popular in the first half of the 18th century.

90

87

89

88

91. An English George III Mahogany Architect's Table, c1765

The main features of this piece are a rising rectangular top adjustable on ratchets and square, chamfered legs with brass scroll brackets and brass castors. It has a frieze drawer fitted with a hinged writing surface and a concealed stationery drawer in the side. Pull-out slides, circular brass candlestands and gilt-metal carrying handles on each side add to the attractiveness of this practical little table, which is of a type produced in quantities too great to have been intended solely for architects, despite the popular name. This one is 2ft 8in (81cm) wide. They are often also referred to as artist's tables, and some are certainly fitted specifically for this purpose, but they are convenient for anyone working with large sheets of paper.

92. An Elaborate English Mahogany Bureau Dressing Chest, c1750

This extraordinary tour-de-force of English cabinetmaking, with its combination of inward and outward curves and heavy mounts, shows German influence but is thought to have been made by the Exeter-born craftsman John Channon. The chest is sophisticated not only in its rococo styling, but also in its design. There are five shaped drawers in the hooded central recess, flanked by two banks of four concave-fronted drawers. The whole of the frieze forms a single shaped drawer. This has a baize-lined slide over fitted compartments. When the drawer is pulled out for writing it is supported on the shaped canted corners which slide forward as an integral part of the drawer. The piece is 5ft 2in (1.58m) wide, and is inlaid with brass and mounted with gilt-brass.

Gilt mounts are rare on English furniture and rococo casting of this quality is rare indeed.

93. An English Mahogany Veneered Bureau Cabinet, c1755

This eccentric piece is also rather large, being 4ft 2½in wide by 7ft 10½in high (1.28 by 2.40m). The upper part is in the form of a four-sided pyramid, with six graduated shelves enclosed by a pair of doors adorned on the inside with mezzotints of great English poets. Beneath this is a fall-flap with a fitted interior behind. The base has eight shallow drawers above and below cupboards decorated on the inside with mezzo-tints of portrait busts of Ancient scholars. The poor quality of the workmanship in this distinctive but rather impractical desk would suggest that it was commissioned from a provincial cabinetmaker, but who dreamed up the design?

93

92

91

94. An American Chippendale Mahogany Kneehole Desk, c1760

This 3ft ½in (93cm) wide desk is known to have been made by John Townsend of Newport, Rhode Island. With the usual complement of long and short drawers around a kneehole cupboard, it is a fine example of the blockfront and shell furniture which was developed by the Townsend and Goddard families of cabinetmakers in the second half of the 18th century. The style later spread to Connecticut, Massachusetts and New York. Reflecting the overall blockfront form, the outer shells are convex and the two central ones are concave.

95. An American Chippendale Mahogany Slope-Front Desk, c1765–75

It has a fitted interior, four long block-fronted drawers and ball-and-claw feet. The blockfronts of Massachusetts pieces like this one tend to extend over all the drawers without any termination, unlike those on Connecticut and Rhode Island pieces which have large carved shell terminations at the top. This example is 3ft 3in (99cm) wide.

96. An American Chippendale Mahogany Slope-Front Desk, c1765–80

3ft 2in (97cm) wide, it is attributed to John Townsend of Newport, Rhode Island. It has a shell-carved blockfront interior of small drawers, pigeonholes and a cupboard. The substantial curved bracket feet are typical of the Townsend style, midway between the simple bracket feet of the Queen Anne period and the showy ball-and-claw feet which characterize the Chippendale period.

97. An American Chippendale Walnut Slope-Front Desk, 1779

This unusual desk has three graduated drawers between fluted quarter-columns at the corners, with a dummy drawer at the top disguising a storage space to which access is gained via a well in the elaborately fitted interior of pigeonholes and drawers. It is 3ft 5½in (1.05m) wide and stands on ogee bracket feet. It is from Pennsylvania and is inlaid with the name Abraham Grof and a date.

97

94

95

96

98. An American Chippendale Mahogany Ox-Bow Fronted Desk, c1792–1796

The ox-bow or reverse-serpentine front to the four long drawers is a gentler version of the blockfront. Both are concave at the centre and convex at each side and both are distinctive American styles. The undulation of the ox-bow front produces an interesting play of light and shade and accentuates the rich figure of the mahogany. This desk bears the maker's label of Stone and Alexander of Boston, Massachusetts. It is 3ft 6in (1.07m) wide.

99. An American Maplewood Desk and Bookcase, c1760–1775

There are three bookshelves behind the arched panel doors of the cabinet, and the fine fitted interior of the writing compartment, with its arcading and serpentine-fronted drawers, is typical of the best East Coast desks. This desk was made in Philadelphia. The fluted pilasters on either side of the central small cupboard slide forward to reveal tall document drawers which might be termed secret if they were not a common feature of 18th-century bureaux from England as well as America. Hidden compartments and locks were much favoured by cabinetmakers fitting out good-quality desks and are always worth looking for. In this example the two small drawers which act as supports for the fall flap are locked by wooden springs released from the drawer below. It has a width of 3ft 4in (1.02m).

100. An American Chippendale Mahogany Bombé Desk and Bookcase, c1760–80

This 3ft 2½in (98cm) wide desk was made in Boston, Massachusetts possibly by John Cogswell. The bombé or kettle base was produced in America as a result of European rococo influence and was particularly favoured by Massachusetts craftsmen, but few pieces come as close to the European models as this desk. European styles usually took several decades to become fashionable in America, and they were generally adapted to suit local taste. This craftsman has given the base a serpentine front as well as a bombé outline and the single mirror-panel door is framed in a free spirit with rocaille work, attenuated pilasters and asymmetric scrolls. The compartment behind the slope front of the desk is fitted with a sweep of stepped drawers flanking a small block- and shell-carved cupboard.

100a. An American Chippendale Period Mahogany Desk-and-Cabinet, c1760

It has a base of four long blockfront drawers with fine decorative brasses and bail handles, supported on acanthus-carved ball-and-claw feet. Behind the fall front is an interior of drawers and pigeonholes with a central shell-carved cupboard flanked by columns with flame-carved finials. The cabinet above, with its swan-neck pediment flanked by eagle finials, has reeded pilasters at each side and is fitted with adjustable shelves beneath a row of pigeonholes. It is 3ft 5in (1.05m) wide, and was made in Boston, Massachusetts.

101. An American Chippendale Cherrywood Desk and Bookcase, c1760–90

This fruitwood desk lacks the sophistication of the best East Coast pieces but is notable for the unusual fitting of the bookcase section. It has a scrolled bonnet top, a fitted writing compartment below the slope-front and four long graduated drawers in the base. The whole piece is 3ft 3in (99cm) wide, but the doors are of different widths; the wider one opens onto pigeonholes, the other onto shelving for books. It is from New London Country, Connecticut.

101

10

99

98

100

1700-1800

102. A French Louis XVI Black Lacquer Bureau Plat

This small, finely-proportioned bureau, which has two chinoiserie-decorated drawers in the frieze, is a good example of the light, graceful, rectilinear style of Louis XVI furniture. The restrained neo-classical ornament of laurel festoons at the corners and rosettes on the frieze, the tapering square-section legs and the simple rectangular top are very different from the curves of the rococo which had characterized high Louis XV style. It is 4ft 2½in (1.28m) wide, and was made by Etienne Levasseur, one of the leading *ébénistes* of the period, who became maître in 1767.

103. A Late Louis XVI Mahogany Veneered Bureau Plat and Gradin

An example of the most sober style of French 18th-century furniture, this desk was made by David Roentgen, and is very different from his earlier intricate marquetry pieces but shows his characteristic attention to detail nevertheless.

The central compartment of the gradin has double doors which slide back into the carcase once they have been opened and the two side cupboards have tambour slides so that the desk can be used with the doors open. The top shelves in each compartment incorporate secret slides for storing papers. The surface of the main desk slides forward and the drawer above the kneehole is fitted with a leather-lined slide over compartments and has a pen drawer in one side. The gradin is fixed by dowels and can be lifted off and the legs unscrew, features which would make the desk much easier to transport. The whole thing is 4ft 10½in wide.

105

102

106

103

104

104. A Sycamore Veneered Secrétaire à Abattant, c1780

This secretaire was made by the German *ébéniste* David Roentgen, with marquetry decoration of wreaths and garlands of flowers suspended on ribbons. The decoration at the centre of the fall front, which encloses a number of small drawers around a tambour-fronted recess, depicts a marquetry bird perched in a ring. Below is a cupboard and the band of guilloche ornament across the frieze above disguises a drawer which springs open at the touch of a button. Such mechanical sophistication was a speciality of this craftsman, who received the title *Ébéniste-Mécanicien du Roi et de la Reine* after supplying a good deal of furniture to the French royal household in the 1770s. Roentgen's workshop was at Neuwied on the Rhine, but he had subsidiary workshops in Berlin and Vienna as well as Paris and supplied furniture to important clients all over Europe. One of a group of German cabinetmakers favoured by Louis XVI and Marie-Antoinette, Roentgen was ruined by the French Revolution, when his Paris stocks were confiscated and his German workshops overrun and looted by Revolutionary soldiers.

105. A French Louis XVI Black Lacquer Secrétaire à Abattant

This lovely piece is inset with panels of Japanese-style *lac burgauté* on the front and sides depicting peacocks and spectacular trailing blooms. This glowing exoticism is contrasted by the typical neo-classical gilt-bronze ornament of the period – a frieze of lozenges, rosettes and garlands across the top drawer, ribbon-tied laurels as escutcheons on the drop-front and the two cupboard doors, rosettes, acanthus leaves and trailing garlands on the canted corners and a bold leaf-framed mask on the apron. It is 3ft 2in (96cm) wide.

106. A French Louis XVI Tulipwood and Marquetry Secrétaire à Rideau

This type of desk, in which shelves and small drawers are concealed behind tambour shutters which slide across like curtains, was never common in France, but a small number are known from this period. Beneath the shutters is a narrow fall-flap disguised as three drawers behind which a leather-lined slide provides the writing surface. In the base is a two-door cupboard decorated with marquetry urns and flowers on a quarter-veneered ground. It is 3ft 3in (99cm) wide, and the rectangular top is marble.

107. A French Black-Lacquered Secrétaire à Abattant with Cabinet and Clock

This now stands in Waddesdon Manor in Buckinghamshire. Its early history remains a mistery, although the 19th-century belief that it was made for Louis XIV has long been discounted. The monumental quality of the piece (it is 5ft 7in (1.07m) wide and 13ft 5in (4.09m) high) is certainly closer to early 18th-century taste than to the mainstream neo-classical style of the 1770s, when it was actually made, and it is likely that it was commissioned from Paris craftsmen for export to a European court. It is stamped with the marks of Jean Goyer (*maître* 1760) and Jacques Dubois, who died in 1763 but whose business was continued by his wife and son using the same *estampille*.

The remarkably elaborate mounts suggest that it was made for a powerful ruler. The bronze eagle perched on a tortoiseshell at the top holds the olive branch of Peace in its beak and the thunderbolts of War in its claws. The allegorical figures on either side balance Force (right) and Magnanimity (left), while the Arts are represented in an oval roundel at the centre of the cabinet doors, here opened to reveal the interior shelves.

The whole of the central section of the upper part contains the weight and pendulum of the huge clock, which strikes on a bell and indicates the time, the day of the week and the day of the month. The second dial at the centre of the writing compartment is a repeater, originally connected to the main movement by a rod.

The fall-front is decorated on the outside with a Japanese lake scene in black and gold lacquer and is counterbalanced by two weights of 35lbs (15.9Kg) each within the carcase. The writing compartment is fitted with drawers and pigeonholes and there are further niches behind the hinged grilles on each side. There are four more drawers behind the double doors in the base which are shown closed.

108. A French Louis XVI Mahogany Secrétaire à Abattant

This is a particularly plain example of Jean-Henri Riesener's undemonstrative style of the 1780s but it may well have been made for the Louvre in Paris as it has royal inventory marks on the back.

There is a frieze drawer beneath the white marble top, a fitted interior behind the fall-flap and a strong-box beneath the double panelled doors in the base. The canted fluted columns with sunflower mounts at the corners are the only elaboration on a piece which relies almost exclusively on the effect of well-chosen veneers. (These are now rather cracked, perhaps due to the overloading of the flap. Many secretaires have come to grief in this way.)

109. A Small French Louis XVI Secrétaire à Abattant

A number of different materials have been used in the construction of this desk: it is marble-topped, veneered in thuyawood, satinwood and purplewood and mounted with classically-inspired gilt-bronze ornament and Sèvres porcelain plaques depicting pastoral courting scenes. The fall-front, which is now supported on struts but was originally balanced by a system of counterweights, conceals an interior of shelves, pigeonholes and drawers which can be lifted out and used as a separate unit. Below the desk is a single frieze drawer decorated with a gilt-bronze panel of putti playing with scientific instruments. This piece bears the stamp of the German *ébéniste* Adam Weisweiler and shows many characteristic features of his work, especially the gilt-bronze caryatids with baskets on their heads, known as *canephori,* at each corner. It is 2ft 6in (76cm) wide.

110. A French Louis XVI Black Lacquer Secrétaire à Abattant, c1780

This 2ft 11in (89cm) wide piece was made by Etienne Levasseur. The upper section has open serpentine shelves at the sides and drawers above and below the fall-front, shown open here to reveal the interior of drawers and shelves in tulipwood and kingwood veneer. The outside of the flap (see detail) is a good example of a fine lacquer panel, imported from Japan and incorporated into a European piece. Here the composition has been used to its best advantage; on earlier pieces of lesser quality the use of imported lacquer can be quite clumsy.

Small secretaires of this type (this one is 2ft 11in (89cm) wide), flanked by small serpentine-fronted shelves and raised on delicate tapering legs, were a popular form towards the end of Louis XV's reign.

109

110

108

107

111. A French Louis XVI Period Bureau à Cylindre

This large desk, 4ft 10in (1.47m) wide, was made by Jean-François Leleu. It is of tulipwood, with restrained neo-classical ormolu mounts. As the leather-lined writing slide is pulled forward the solid cylinder front rolls back to reveal a fitted interior of small drawers. There are three further drawers in the frieze. Leleu became *maître* in 1764, having trained in the workshops of J-F Oeben, where he would have worked on the great Bureau du Roi. The flamboyance of that desk belonged to the earlier 18th century but it was one of the first to have the cylinder front, a feature fully developed here by Leleu in the sterner neo-classical style of the last quarter of the century.

112. A French Bureau à Cylindre of the Louis XVI period

The most immediately striking freature about this desk is the particularly rich ormolu decoration on the tulipwood in the form of entrelac, rosettes and stylized leaf borders and unusual ring handles. The solid cylinder front is panelled with a central parquetry medallion and conceals three drawers. Beneath it is a pull-out writing slide with ormolu knobs and three frieze drawers, one of which is reinforced as a *coffre fort* for the storage of valuables. Above the writing compartment is a marble-topped *gradin* of three drawers with a gallery. The desk is 3ft 2in (96.5cm) wide. Elegant cylinder desks of this type superseded the more basic slope-front desks in fashionable circles in the second half of the 18th century.

113. A late 18th-century Bureau à Cylindre

The desk, 3ft 2½in (98cm) wide, was reputedly made for Tsar Paul I of Russia by the German *ébéniste*, David Roentgen, but is now in Anglesey Abbey in Cambridgeshire. The inlaid Russian townscapes on the cylinder, drawer-fronts and side panels are typical of the high quality of marquetry work which helped to make Roentgen's workshops at Nieuwied famous all over Europe.

113

111

112

114. A French Amaranth, Tulipwood and Parquetry Bureau en Pente of the Early Louis XVI Period

It bears the stamp of Pierre Boichod, an *ébéniste* who became *maître* in 1769. Beneath the shallow slope-front, which is bordered with a wide gilt-bronze band cast with flowerheads, the interior is fitted with drawers and inlaid with sprays of flowers. There are no drawers in the urn-decorated frieze and access to the considerable storage space behind it is through a lidded well in the bottom of the writing compartment. Thus a single key secures the whole. Small bureaux of this kind (it is only 2ft 11in (64cm) wide) are often known as bureaux de dame, but slope-front examples are more common in Louis XV style.

115. A French Early Louis XVI Table à Écrire

Only 1ft 7in (48cm) wide, this little writing table is fitted with a frieze drawer containing a leather-lined flap and a pen tray. Beneath is a tambour slide concealing three more drawers. The overall decoration is trellis and Greek key parquetry, ormolu mounts and slender cabriole legs. It is stamped for Léonard Boudin, who became *maître* in 1761. The Greek key inlay and rather formal classically-inspired mounts would have been fashionable elements, married to the more sinuous lines of the rococo-inspired cabriole legs.

114

115

116

116. An Ebony Bureau de Dame by Adam Weisweiler

The gilt-bronze legs are in the form of caryatids with flower baskets on their heads and the interlaced stretcher, a typical feaure of Weisweiler's work, is mounted with a central gilt-bronze basket. It is only 1ft 6½in (47cm) wide, with an adjustable reading slope made from a panel of Japanese lacquer.

This is one of a group of similar pieces made by Weisweiler for the Château de Saint Cloud, just outside Paris, which was bought by Louis XVI from the Duc d'Orléans in 1785. The desk was installed in the private apartment of Queen Marie Antoinette, who, as the daugher of the Austrian Empress Maria Theresa, tended to favour *ébénistes* of Germanic origin like Riesener and Weisweiler. The latter began his career in the workshops of David Roentgen at Neuwied on the Rhine, and arrived in Paris at about the time that Louis XVI came to the throne in 1774. He became a *maître ébéniste* in 1778 and supplied a good deal of furniture to the royal palaces, including this desk, through the agency of the furniture dealer Dominique Daguerre.

The extensive gilt-bronze work on this desk has been attributed to Pierre Gouthière, the most celebrated *ciseleur* of the time.

117. A French Louis XVI Kingwood Secrétaire Commode

This desk is decorated with chequered parquetry surrounds on the sides and on the two-drawer *sans traverse* base. The writing compartment below the white marble top is simply fitted and has an interesting leather-lined surface which drops forward on hinges and can then be pulled out further to give more room for papers. Secretaires of this kind were much less common in France than in England. This piece is 4ft (1.22m) wide.

118. An Unusual French Table à Gradin in Mahogany by Jean Henri Riesener, *c*1790

The galleried gradin itself holds three small drawers and there are a writing slide and further drawers in the frieze. This small desk, only 1ft 9in (53cm) in diameter, is a sobre reflection of the post-Revolutionary times. Riesener survived the Terror, despite having been a favourite of Marie-Antoinette; but the furniture produced by his workshop never rivalled the masterpieces of earlier years, not least because there were precious few clients left with money to spend on very expensive pieces.

119. A French Louis XVI Tulipwood Bonheur-du-Jour

The overall decoration is trellis parquetry with flowerheads in each diamond. The legs are plain square tapers and the apparent fluting is simulated by an inlay of lighter wood shading to dark. The upper section, topped by a three-quarter gilt gallery, is enclosed by a tambour slide which opens from left to right. The base consists of one long and two short drawers and is fitted with a pull-out slide. The undertier, as well as being a useful place for keeping sewing or other items that might be needed at a moment's notice, acts as a stretcher for the delicate legs. This is a relatively unsophisticated but highly practical example of one of the most popular of all ladies' desk designs. It is 2ft 1¾in (65.5cm) wide.

118

119

117

120. An Unusual English Satinwood and Marquetry Half-Round Writing Commode in Adam style

This commode dates from the mid-1770s and *4ft 3in (1.30m) wide.* The central section, flanked by cupboards, contains three long drawers beneath a writing drawer which is concealed behind herringbone-veneered tambour slides. The writing compartment is fitted with an inkwell, small drawers and a central cupboard inset with a small clock.

The inclusion of a writing drawer in a commode of this type is rare, but the form and decoration of the piece are typical of the delicately neo-classical style that was very influential in England in the 1770s following the lead of Robert Adam and his brother James. Adam was an architect who aimed to create a harmonious relationship between furniture and the room that contained it; he was involved in the design of every detail of the house, from doorknobs to firegrates. His furniture was generally fairly severe in design but lightened by the use of delicate and airy classical motifs. The inlaid urns, honeysuckle, scrolls and trailing garryah flowers which adorn the drawer-fronts are typical.

Adam's neo-classical style was much spare and lighter than the Palladian style popularised by William Kent and others in the second quarter of the 18th century, and less seriously imitative than the classical revival inspired by Thomas Hope in the early 19th century.

121. An English Tulipwood Bonheur-du-Jour, *c1775*

The neo-classical marquetry decoration is in the Adam style. The upper section contains two small cupboards with oval paterae on the doors and a single shelf with a three-quarter brass gallery, while the serpentine main section is decorated around the frieze with stylised flowers and festoons and contains a single drawer. This piece is 2ft 11½in (90cm) wide.

The bonheur-du-jour began to appear in British homes after its great popularity in France.

122

123

121

120

122. An English George III Mahogany Tambour Desk and Bookcase, Late 18th Century

This is 3ft 7½in (1.10m) wide, with a base of four long graduated drawers on splayed or French feet, a fitted writing compartment with a slide and a bookrest, and a lancet-arch glazed bookcase. The tambour slide, formed from strips of wood with a canvas backing running in grooves, was a feature first introduced to Britain from France in the late 18th century and is illustrated in several of the pattern books of the 1780s and '90s. However, in his *Cabinet Dictionary* of 1803, Sheraton remarks that "The writing tambour tables are almost out of use at present, being both insecure, and very liable to injury". The tambour is certainly much more delicate than the simple fall-front, and also prone to jamming if not made to the highest standards. It is noticeable that makers almost invariably fitted two handles on tambour slides and even on solid cylinder fronts in an effort to encourage the user to open them with two hands and thus avoid undue pressure on one side.

123. An English George III Mahogany Tambour Desk

The whole desk is plain but for some geometric ebonised stringing. It is fitted with drawers and pigeonholes behind the shutter, which rolls back into the body of the desk. The pull-out slide incorporates a hinged bookrest with a baize lining and there is a pair of drawers below.

This light and elegant writing desk on slim tapering legs with spade feet is a good example of the more delicate style of furniture fashionable in England during the late 18th and early 19th centuries. It is very similar to a "Tambour Writing Table" illustrated in Hepplewhite's *The Cabinet-Maker and Upholster's Guide* published in 1788, but the stringing might suggest a later date. It is 3ft 7in (1.10m) wide.

124. An English Library Writing Table, *c*1771

This was made by Thomas Chippendale for Harewood House near Leeds.

The leather-lined top, 6ft 9½in (2.07m) wide, is supported on two massive pedestals, each with three graduated drawers behind a cupboard door on one side and a partitioned cupboard on the other. There are three drawers in the frieze on one side and a central dummy flanked by true drawers on the other. It is veneered in rosewood with engraved marquetry decoration in neo-classical style; the frieze with a band of linked rosette medallions, the four cupboard doors with vases topped by anthemion and festooned with husks. The insides of the drawers and doors are veneered in rosewood of a deep brown which would have originally matched the now faded exterior. Two hundred years ago the contrast between the light tones of the beech, tulipwood, satinwood, sycamore and holly marquetry and the darker tones of the main body would have been much more striking; nevertheless the desk, with its finely-made mounts of gilt bronze, remains a fine example of Chippendale's work under the influence of Robert Adam. It is important to realise that the rococo, gothic and Chinese styles usually associated with the name of Chippendale were a mid-century fashion. By the 1770s Chippendale's firm was supplying fashionable neo-classical furniture as part of his overall interior decoration service, and many of the finest and best-documented pieces are in this style.

125. An English George III Mahogany Breakfront Secretaire-Bookcase

This bookcase has four glazed bookcase doors in the upper section and three panelled cupboards in the base. The two doors at the ends enclose three drawers each, with a further deep drawer above to match the wide secretaire drawer in the centre which pulls out and has a fall-front for writing. Large library pieces fitted for writing like this one (8ft 9in (2.67m) wide) were very popular towards the end of the 18th century and were produced in large numbers.

126. An English Breakfront Secretaire-Bookcase of the 1780s or '90s

This beautiful piece is 4ft 4in (1.32m) wide and is veneered in satinwood with marquetry decoration in holly, harewood, tulipwood, ebony and pear, and with painted honeysuckle decoration along the scalloped cornice. Below the trellis-glazed cupboards are three deep drawers inlaid with a central patera and hanging garlands of flowers. The central drawer pulls out and is fitted with drawers and pigeonholes behind the green baize-lined fall front. Below are three long drawers, flanked by small cupboards with urn and swag inlay, and the bookcase stands on six tapered feet with simulated fluting. Elegant satinwood furniture of this kind has popularly been associated with Thomas Sheraton, but he made no specifically identifiable furniture and his *Drawing Book* of 1791 was really a reflection of the delicate neo-classical tastes of the time. As he wrote himself, his book was 'intended to exhibit the present taste of furniture, and at the same time to give the workman some assistance in the manufacturing part of it'.

127. An American Federal Period Mahogany-Veneered Secretary and Bookcase

Although this scroll-top writing desk owes a debt to the Chippendale style of pre-Revolutionary America, it also anticipates several features of the desks of the later Federal period. It was made in Salem, Massachusetts, during the last 20 years of the 18th century. The rosette-carved scroll pediment is a slimmed-down and elegant affair centred by a classical urn, and the relatively low upper section is a foretaste of the fashionable dwarf cabinets of the early 19th century. The top drawer of the serpentine four-drawer base is in fact a pull-out writing compartment with a fall-front, itself an innovation of the later 18th century. Inside it is fitted with small drawers, one carved with a fan, and a hidden compartment. Its width is 3ft 8½in (1.13m).

127

125

124

126

128. A Late-18th-Century English Mahogany and Satinwood Partners' Desk

Partners' desks are so called because they have drawers in both sides, the idea being that business partners could sit facing one another. This desk, 5ft 1in (1.55m), has three frieze drawers and six pedestals drawers in one side, with three frieze drawers and pedestal cupboards in the other. Whether they were used in the library, the study or in an office, they were intended to stand in the middle of the room rather than against a wall.

129. An English Harlequin Writing and Dressing Table of the 1790s
Shown open and closed.

Based fairly closely on designs published in the *Cabinet-Maker's London Book of Prices* in 1788, this table has a two-flap top which folds out to the sides to rest on supporting lopers. Underneath is a leather writing surface and a bank of drawers and pigeonholes which rises on two coil springs and can be fixed in position. It is 2ft 1in (64cm) wide when closed. Of the two drawers in the main body of the table the top one is a dummy and the second a dressing drawer fitted with an adjustable looking-glass. Below the drawers are double tambour slides made up of alternate strips of mahogany and harewood. This pattern continues around the base while the rest of the table is veneered in mahogany, crossbanded with tulipwood and with boxwood stringing.

130. A Writing Cabinet, c1800

This is a London-made multi-purpose piece of furniture, 3ft 4in (1.01m) wide, veneered in satinwood and sabicu with ebony stringing. It comprises a three-part glazed display case and a base with two long fitted drawers over a two-door cupboard. The lower of the two drawers, shown open here, is equipped for use when dressing, with a central adjustable mirror and, on either side, six wells with silver-topped bottles, three ivory boxes, a hairbrush, a pincushion and various other lidded compartments. Above this is a fall-front secretaire drawer with a leather writing surface and six small ivory-handled drawers, one of which holds a silver-mounted inkwell and a pounce pot. The shaped pediment incorporates a clock flanked by eight brass campana-shaped candleholders. The clock is inscribed *Week's Museum, Titchborne Street*, a reference to Thomas Weeks's museum of mechanical curiosities which opened at 3–4 Titchborne Street in the late 1790s. This seems to have been the source of the 20 or more cabinets of this type which are known to

survive. The museum exhibited a variety of strange automata, including a 115-piece steel tarantula, and the spirit of the place is reflected in the fact that many of the cabinets were fitted with an automatic barrel organ in the base, connected to the striking mechanism of the clock and playing a variety of tunes. The maker of this cabinet is unknown, but the design owes a debt to Sheraton's *Drawing Book* of 1791, adapted to echo the façade of the museum itself.

130

129

128

131. An English Satinwood Work and Writing Table, c1795

A hinged leather-lined flap folds forward over the dummy drawer in the front and there is a sewing drawer in the side with a hanging bag for storing sewing materials. The book tray above has one long and two short drawers in the base. This piece is only 1ft 9in (54cm) wide. Such pieces often have a detachable book tray fitted with a large bow handle, and are then known as cheverets.

132. An English Mahogany Kidney Writing Table, c1800

Writing and sewing tables featuring the kidney or horseshoe shape first became popular around the middle of the 18th century, and examples are illustrated in cabinetmakers' pattern books from Chippendale onwards. This basic, practical shape, with sides curving around the writer, is often augmented by the provision of a writing slope and compartments in the drawer, or an adjustable slope rising from the centre of the table itself. This is a small example, 2ft 11½in (90cm) wide, with a leather-lined top and a single frieze drawer.

133. An Anglo-Indian Miniature Bureau Cabinet

This enchanting piece, with its veneer of intricately engraved ivory was made in the last quarter of the 18th century by Indian craftsmen for the British market. It is only 1ft 11½in (60cm) wide, with a fitted interior behind the fall front and various lidded compartments and bottles in the large fitted drawer in the base. In the low superstructure above are further small drawers and two cupboards, all decorated like the base, with flowers, fruit and leaves in a continuous band.

134. An English George III Clerk's Desk in Mahogany

The leather-inlaid writing slope forms the hinged lid to a compartment containing two small drawers, and there is a full-width drawer and a shaped gallery in the base. Tall sloping desks of this kind, developments of the simple table desk of the 16th and 17th centuries, continued to be a standard design for clerks throughout the 19th century. Desks of similar design are still to be found in some schools today. This one is 1ft 11in (58cm) wide.

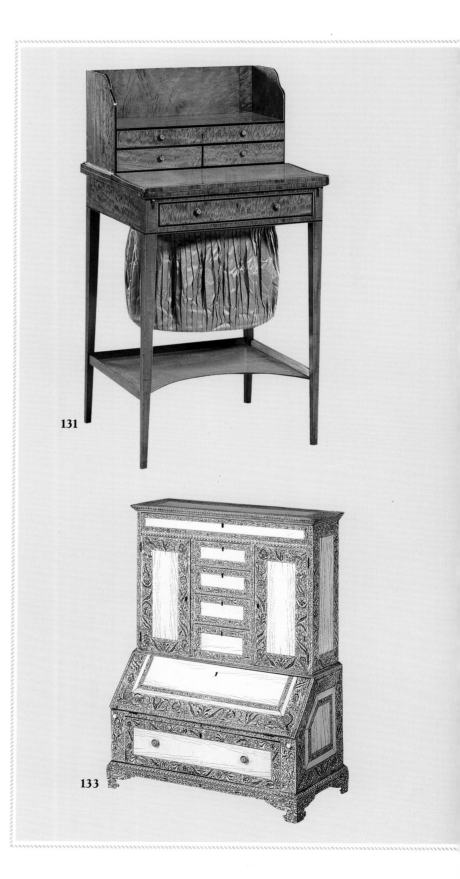

131

133

132

134

1800 TO 1900

This portrait of a late-19th century gentleman in his study by the French artist Gustave Bourgain is intended to project the taste and interests of the sitter, but it also reveals something about the general attitude to furniture styles at the time. He sits at a massive desk on a turned underframe, a 19th-century evocation of 17th-century style adapted for convenience. The geometrically carved chest, the massive throne-like chair in Renaissance style and the primitive stick chair in the foreground are more picturesque reminders of the past. The only piece which owes no debt to the past is the conspicuously comfortable sofa, heavily upholstered and interior-sprung. Such luxury was a 19th-century innovation.

For the furniture historian the 19th century is much more bewildering than the one which preceded it. It was a century when people were more conscious of fashion and of improvements in design and innovations reached a far wider public than had ever been the case before.

The general optimism of the age is most easily detected in the wonderful displays of mechanical progress seen at the big international exhibitions of the second half of the century, but faith in the possibility of improvement is evident much earlier.

Rudolph Ackerman's monthly fashion magazine *The Repository of Arts, Literature, Commerce, Manufactures, Fashions and Politics*, first appeared in 1809 to cater for an increasingly fashion-conscious public. Writing in an early issue in April 1814, he imparted a particular progressive energy to the description of a Carlton House table and chair, named, 'as we presume, from having been first made for the august personage whose correct taste has so classically embellished that beautiful palace'. The compliment to the Prince Regent and his decorative schemes at Carlton House is also an excuse for a more general comment on the responsibility of fashion leaders for 'improving public taste'. He writes: 'To the credit of our higher classes who encourage and of our manufacturers who produce, we now universally quit the overcharged magnificence of former ages, and seek purer models of simplicity and tasteful ornament in every article of daily call. The table and chair which are the subject of the present engraving, are peculiarly of the description of improvement of which we are speaking. They exhibit a judicious combination of elegance and usefulness . . .'

The 19th century did not, of course, escape without piling more than its fair share of 'overcharged magnificence' onto humble desks, cabinets and tables, but the simpler ornament that Ackerman referred to was characteristic of the first three decades of the century, reflected in the Regency style in Britain, the Empire style in France and the Federal style in the newly independent United States. Furniture of this period tended to be more massive and more severely classical than the Adam and Sheraton styles which had preceded it in Britain or the Louis XVI style in France.

In London the publication of Thomas Hope's *Household Furniture and Interior Decoration* in 1807 was influential in introducing a much more archaeologically correct 'Greek style' which modified the form as well as the ornament of furniture.

In France, Napoleon's new regime took to the severely classical forms that emerged as a result of the new archaeological discoveries. They were sufficiently different from the trappings of the displaced monarchy and its austerity suited a country impoverished by revolution and war. After the Directoire period in the 1790s, the style lost some of its austerity but preserved a glossy appearance together with masculine, commanding forms suited to the new order. The new sleek styles depended on correct proportion for their effect and in France the secrétaire à abattant usually took on an uncompromising architectural form with flanking columns and a simple pediment. The large area of the flap when closed in the vertical position contributed to the overall uncluttered effect. For the same reason the secretaire drawer or a fitted pull-out slide were favourite Regency solutions in Britain, being neat and unobtrusive when not in use.

On both sides of the Channel dark and opulent veneers were fashionable, frequently set off by small amounts of bright metalwork – classically inspired gilt mounts being the norm in France, brass inlay in Britain.

The Empire style became international, through imitation and through the influence of Napoleon's relatives, set up as heads of state in Scandinavia, Holland, Germany, Italy and Spain, the bulwarks of the short-lived Empire.

In the United States both Regency and Empire styles influenced fashionable cabinetmakers who found in the serious classical forms a suitable reflection of the aspirations of the new republic. A heavier, more classical style continued to be popular in America until the mid-century, but it had to compete with the influence of the host of revivalist styles which began to dominate European design after the 1820s.

The European revivals of this period were all far less exacting than the Hope-inspired Regency classicism had been. In England Louis XIV became popular, but Gothic and Elizabethan were current at the same time and it was often thought suitable to use different styles for different rooms, or even to mix them. In France, during the 1830s, rococo came back into fashion and remained influential to the end of a century that saw several other Louis Revivals.

In America Gothic, Rococo, Renaissance and Elizabethan styles all had vogues before the influence of the European Arts and Crafts movements ushered in the modern age. The many confusing revivals of the Victorian era seem ill-suited to a progressive age, but in American especially, it is possible to see the forward drive. In the Mid-Western States – Indiana, Illinois, Ohio – where timber and transport routes were close at hand, veritable furniture factories sprang up to provide comfortable, respectable surroundings for a growing nation. In the 1860s there were no fewer than 18 factories producing furniture in Chicago alone.

The results were not always the 'judicious combinations of elegance and usefulness' that so pleased the eye of Thomas Hope and Rudolph Ackerman, but they were often triumphs of a mechanical age. The great international exhibitions of the 19th century were not generally noted for their pure design and good taste, quite the reverse, but they were rightful celebrations of technology, of the bandsaws, scrapers, moulding machines, polishing machines, and planing machines to be found in the industrial rather than the decorative arts pavilions.

These had a profound effect on furniture design, for in the 20th century these industrial methods began to dictate styles of their own.

135. An Early 19th-Century Gilt Bronze Mounted Mahogany Table à la Tronchin

This desk is obviously French in style but is in fact probably of Scandinavian or German origin. The baize-lined top is adjustable to any angle and can be raised to a convenient height on the four corner supports, which slide down into the legs as the top is lowered. There are two drawers and two slides in the frieze. The table is named after Théodore Tronchin (1709–81), a Swiss doctor who was a strong advocate of fresh air and exercise, good posture and loose-fitting clothes. In the 1770s he ordered an adjustable table of the type illustrated here, apparently because he felt it was more natural to read and write in a standing position. His desk was raised and lowered by means of a handle at the side and this system is seen on many example. Although the table has taken his name he did not invent it, and in Britain such pieces are generally known as architect's tables.

136. A French Empire Mahogany Secrétaire à Abattant

The black marble top, 3ft 2in (96cm) wide, is a large fall-front with a fitted interior behind and a pair of cupboard doors in the base. The bold square lines of the secrétaire à abattant were well suited to the aspirations of Napoleon's years of success, and this is a good example of the use of large expanses of veneer with fine figure, set off by small and often highly-classical mounts in gilt bronze. Here the escutcheon on the drawer is flanked by a pair of winged angels in loose drapes and stylised torches are placed either side of the main desk. The influence of the French Empire spread this style right across Europe, from Italy to Scandinavia.

138

136

137

135

137. An Early 19th-Century Secrétaire à Abattant

The fall-front writing compartment has one drawer above and three below, and the whole is flanked by reeded columns with gilt capitals, bases and bands. The spectacularly colourful flower decoration is formed from pieces of plain and stained mother-of-pearl set in black lacquer, a technique known as *lac burgauté*, and the desk probably originates from one of the Dutch Far Eastern colonies. It is 3ft 6in (1.07m) wide.

138. An Early 19th-Century Russian Writing Cabinet

This remarkable piece is only 3ft 1in (94cm) wide but 9ft 2in (2.80m) high to the top of the double bird's head finial on the dome. Conceived in neo-classical vein, it is veneered in Karelian birch and poplar, woods generally found only on Russian pieces. Beneath a clock in the upper section is a cupboard with a classical figure in gilt bronze in a niche on the door. The cupboard is flanked by two pairs of white marble and gilt bronze columns, and beneath is a drawer with a fold-down front. Behind the leather-lined fall-front the writing compartment is fitted with small drawers and pigeonholes built in the same style as the exterior, with white marble columns flanking a mirror-backed central niche over an area of simulated brickwork. The base is a simple two-door cupboard.

139. An English Regency Carlton House Desk

This mahogany desk, 5ft 1½in (1.61m) wide, is on ribbed tapering legs with castors at the feet and carved paterae at the heads. There is a brass gallery around the top, and the gilt bail handles are in the form of looped drapery. This example has a bank of six drawers in the superstructure, with two cupboards (one with a slot for posting letters in the top, probably for incoming mail) and two more drawers in the curved sloping wings, but many variations of this distinctive and practical design are to be found. In some cases the wings are stepped rather than sloping and in others they continue round at the same height as the back. An adjustable slope for writing is also a common feature.

The type first appeared in the late 18th century and continued to be popular during the Regency period. Edwardian examples in the same style are also found.

140. An English Regency Mahogany Carlton House Desk

This is a good example of the influence of Greek, Roman and Egyptian antiquity on furniture design during the early years of the 19th century. The leather-lined writing slope is flanked by small drawers with gilt-bronze lion's head handles, the frieze is inset with Sphinx busts, and the moulding of the legs, which rest on brass paw feet, derives from a classical motif of a bundle of reeds. The whole desk is 3ft 7in (1.89m) wide.

141. An English Regency Carlton House Desk

The distinctive D-shape of this writing table puts it firmly in the Carlton House family, but the massive flanking pillars in the form of fasces are most unusual; they stand on ebonised feet carved with two tiers of lotuses and serve as cupboards, secured, like all the drawers, with Bramah locks. The circular tops are inlaid with compass medallions.

Maritime decorative motifs, like the dolphin handles on the main drawers, became popular after Nelson's naval victory at Trafalgar in 1805. This desk is made of mahogany with gilt edging and handles, 4ft 9in (1.45m) wide.

139

142

140

141

142. An English George IV Mahogany Kneehole Desk of the 1820s

This desk, 4ft 10½in (1.49m) wide, boasts some interesting mechanical features. On each side of the kneehole there are three drawers with ebonised stringing and turned ebonised knobs, but the top drawer on each side is a dummy containing the mechanism for cranking up the superstructure of five cupboards and for lowering it into the body of the desk when not in use. The central writing slope is hinged, with storage space underneath. Desks with rising banks of drawers or cupboards are often referred to as 'harlequins', perhaps because the superstructure springs up like a harlequin, or because it disappears like a harlequin.

143. An Early-19th-Century English Regency Secretaire-Cabinet

The main decoration on this piece (2ft 6in (76cm) wide) is satinwood stringing. It has a fitted fall-front writing drawer over a cupboard with brass grille doors in the base. The low glazed cupboard in the superstructure, without the architectural pediment and cornice which had been a normal feature during the previous century, is typical of the smaller cabinets that became fashionable during the Regency period. The use of latticework backed by fabric is also characteristic of the lighter approach of the period.

144. One of a Pair of English Regency Rosewood Secretaires

The open shelving rests on turned gilt-bronze supports with X-shaped inserts. The base is 3ft 1½in (96cm) wide with a deep writing drawer over a two-door cupboard with metal grille fronts, backed with fabric.

The use of exotic, deeply-figured veneers outlined by gilt-bronze beading was much favoured during the Regency period, and small secretaires or cylinder desks were generally preferred to the more imposing slope-front bureau-bookcases which continued to be made by country craftsmen. It is unusual to find desks made in pairs from any period.

145. An English Regency Rosewood Lady's Writing and Sewing Table

The body rests on ring-turned taper legs with castors. It has an adjustable reading stand hinged along the front edge, a pull-out writing slide above a dummy drawer in the front, and a drawer at the side fitted for writing accessories. The pleated bag underneath is for storing sewing materials and the matching screen at the back slides up and down so that the desk can be placed close to the fire while the woman's complexion is protected from the heat.

146. A Small Regency Mahogany Writing Table, c1815

This writing table was made in the manner of Thomas Hope, and has a drawer fitted with an adjustable writing slope, a pen tray and compartments. The lion's head and ring handles, the brass paw feet and the delicately shaped and reeded legs are all typical of the austere classical style which Hope introduced with the publication of his *Household Furniture and Interior Decoration* of 1807.

146

145

143

144

147. An English Regency Mahogany Library Desk

This piece (4ft 7in (1.04m) wide) is conceived in French Empire taste with plain panels at the ends centred by gilt-bronze Bacchic masks and flanked by free-standing reeded columns at the corners. It has open folio racks below a green leather-lined top with a matching slide.

148. An English Regency Mahogany Library Table

This large writing desk (6ft 3½in (1.12m) across), with three drawers in each side of the frieze, is designed to stand in the centre of a library. It is banded with satinwood and boxwood stringing and supported on four ring-turned tapering legs with brass castors. Its unadorned elegance is a good example of the sterner side of Regency design, ideally suited to the library and very different from some of the exotic creations of the period commissioned by the Regent himself for the Brighton Pavilion representing the other extreme.

149. An English Regency Mahogany Library Writing table

This typical Regency design, similar to the sofa table but without its drop end-flaps, is strung with boxwood and ebony. The lionhead and ring handles and heavy scrolled supports acknowledge the severe Greek taste made popular by the pattern books of Thomas Hope and George Smith. The main body is on end-supports joined by a single stretcher and is 4ft (1.22m) wide.

150. An English Regency Mahogany Writing Table

This is known to have been one of a pair supplied in 1811 by Gillows of Lancaster and described as 'mahogany chamber writing tables, reeded legs and rails beaded as common'. They were intended for bedrooms and are typical of the standard Regency output of this firm, who were the leading cabinetmakers outside London in the 18th and 19th centuries and among the first to regularly stamp their furniture. This desk is 3ft (91cm) wide, with two frieze drawers and a lidded well containing a pen tray and bottle holders in the top.

148

150

149

147

151. An American Federal Period Mahogany Tambour Desk

This desk is 3ft 1½in (95cm) wide, and was probably made in New Hampshire in the late 18th or early 19th century. The upper section is delicately inlaid with chequered lining and contains a central cupboard with two inner drawers, flanked by sliding tambour shutters. In front of this is a hinged flap which folds out to form a writing surface supported on lopers and there are four long graduated drawers in the base.

The low superstructure of this piece reflects the European fashion for smaller, more elegant desks during the same period, but the combination of tambour shutters and a fold-out writing surface on a chest of drawers is one of the most distinctive original forms of the Federal period.

152. An American Federal Mahogany Secretary and bookcase

This is known to have been made by Ebenezer Eustis of Salem, Massachusetts and dated 1808. Of imposing proportions, 5ft 4in (1.62cm) wide, it comprises drawers, cupboards and a central desk drawer in the lower section, upon which rests the glazed bookcase. The bookcase top is slightly receded from the unit below – a characteristic Sheraton feature – and the flat surfaces, delicate line inlays and peg-top feet all reflect the English style of the period. The pediment with its brass eagle and urn finials is an American touch. Sometimes known as Salem secretaries, large Sheraton-style pieces of this type are one of the distinctive forms of the Federal period.

153

154

151

153. An American Federal Mahogany Butler's Desk, c1810

This desk is 3ft 11in (1.20m) wide, and was probably made in Philadelphia or New York. The two curved sides each contain a two-handled drawer over a cupboard, while the breakfront centre section holds a shallow drawer over a pull-out writing drawer and a two-door cupboard. The writing comparment is fitted with three satinwood drawers.

154. An American Pine Slant-Front Desk

This simple four-drawer desk, hand-painted with brightly-coloured birds, flowers, hearts and other traditional motifs as well as paterae and stars in imitation of more sophisticated pieces, is a reminder that by no means all 19th-century furniture was produced in mainstream styles.

It was made in Mahantango Valley, Schuylkill County, Pennsylvania, 3ft 6¾in (1.09m) wide. Expatriate communities, isolated by terrain or by choice, continued to produce their own distinctive forms, sometimes long after they had become old-fashioned in their countries of origin. The painted decoration here continues the traditions of the Pennsylvanian Germans (sometimes known as Pennsylvanian Dutch) who settled in large numbers in the South East of the state.

152

89

155. A Viennese Mahogany Secrétaire à Abattant, c1820

The inverted pear-shaped body, 3ft 7in (1.09m) wide, is fitted with a semi-circular drawer at the top with a fan-carved fall front. Below it is another shallow drawer and there are two more drawers below the main flap as well as one in the low platform. The whole desk is gilded and supported on massive lion-paw feet. The writing compartment, concealed behind a shaped fall, contains an architectural arrangement of drawers around a mirrored temple interior with secret drawers.

Elaborate and eccentrically shaped secrétaires such as this example were based on French Empire style, but they were an Austrian and German speciality. Plainer examples in Biedermeier style often have a surprisingly modern, almost Art Deco look, but the use of classical acanthus and egg-and-dart moulding ties this piece to the early 19th century.

156. A North German Secretaire in Biedermeier style, c1820

The exterior of this desk is birch-veneered with a fitted interior in contrasting dark mahogany veneer. It is of typical architectural form and shown here as it was intended to be seen, the focal point of a domestic interior. Like the other pieces in the room it is characterized by strong form, light colour and minimal applied ornament.

157. A mid-19th Century French Walnut Bureau à Cylindre of the Louis Philippe period

This bureau is 4ft 11in (1.50m) wide, with a solid cylinder front which rolls back to reveal a fitted interior and a leather-lined writing slide. This solid and heavy reinterpretation of the Louis XVI cylinder bureau has three drawers above the desk and nine drawers below, including three in the frieze.

155

157

158. A French Mid-19th-Century Bonheur-du-Jour

This fine quality piece is of ebony decorated with lacquer, gilt metal mounts and pewter stringing in the manner of the late 18th-century *ébéniste* Adam Weisweiler. It is mounted with Japanese lacquer panels, having shelved cupboards in the superstructure and a secretaire drawer in the base fitted with a leather-lined writing surface and four small compartments, and measures 2ft 7in (79cm) wide. It bears the mark of Prosper Guillaume Durand, who, with his father, made furniture for various royal palaces in the 1830s and became *ébéniste du roi* under Louis Philippe in 1839. His business flourished until the 1860s, producing *meubles de luxe* in Louis XVI style.

159. A French Kingwood Veneered Secrétaire à Abattant of the 1860s

This secretaire is 2ft 8in (43cm) wide, with a fall-front writing compartment decorated with a black and gilt lacquered chinoiserie scene and a two-door cupboard decorated with a pair of painted ribbon-tied bouquets. It bears the burnt-in mark of Alfred Beurdeley, the last principal of a family firm that specialised in producing high-quality furniture in 18th-century styles, following the Parisian taste for the many 'Louis Revivals' of the 19th century. This rather stolid-looking desk draws on the late Louis XV period for inspiration only, but the Beurdeley workshops, like many leading Paris cabinetmakers of the time, also produced excellent copies of 18th century pieces.

160. A Mid-19th-Century French Bonheur-du-Jour

The galleried superstructure of serpentine shelves flanking a cupboard are decorated with marquetry birds on an ebony ground. There are three serpentine-fronted drawers below, one of which contains an inkstand. The shaped stand contains a single drawer and a slide and is similarly decorated with flower marquetry on an ebony ground. It measures 2ft 9in (84cm) across. This is a typically eclectic 19th-century product displaying elements from several different 18th-century styles. The bonheur-du-jour is essentially a post-1750 form but it is seen here in an exaggerated rococo style with heavy mounts and elaborate marquetry cartouches of leafy scrolls.

159

161

161. A French Bureau à Gradin, c1860

Profusely mounted with gilt bronzes of the highest quality and inset with black and gold chinoiserie lacquer panels, this 19th-century creation was inspired by the rococo masterpieces of over a century before. Few 18th-century pieces, however, achieved the easy opulence seen here. It is but a short step from these sinuous leafy mounts stretching up from the legs and terminating in double candleholders, to the wholly organic treatment of desks by the Art Nouveau craftsmen of the last quarter of the century. The natural sweep of the *gradin* itself is also forward-looking, but the central clock with its bronze putti supporters is pure 18th-century rococo. It is 5ft 3in (1.60m) wide, with six small shaped drawers in the gradin and two larger drawers in the frieze.

160

158

162. A French Napoleon III Kingwood, Tulipwood and Marquetry Bonheur-du-Jour of the Mid-19th Century

The superstructure consists of a two-door cupboard and two drawers topped by a gilt-brass gallery and a frieze drawer fitted with a velvet-lined slide. Almost every surface of this Louis XV revival desk is decorated with a pattern of continuous floral scrolls of rather uninspired form, but there are two 'show panels' of high-quality marquetry in the shaped ebonised reserves on the cupboard doors. Like much of the 18th century style furniture which filled wealthy French homes in the 19th century, this desk shows an enthusiasm for the decorative quality of the rococo but does not quite recapture the poise and balance of the earlier age. It is 2ft 7½in (79cm) wide. The best 19th-century French reproduction furniture is very hard to distinguish from 18th century originals, however.

163. A Secretaire-Cabinet, 1860s

Shown open and closed.

This remarkable piece was presumably made for the French market, but is mounted inside and out with Dresden painted porcelain plaques. Most of the plaques show lovers in landscapes painted in the manner of Watteau, but at the centre of the swan neck pediment at the top is a small oval portrait of Marie-Amelie, the wife of Louis-Philippe of France. When the doors of the cabinet are opened, her portrait appears superimposed on a large circular portrait of the emperor himself in a full-bottomed wig and armour. The interior of the cabinet is fitted with numerous porcelain-mounted drawers grouped around a central cupboard, and below this is a fall-front writing drawer with chequerboard inlay. In the base is a serpentine-fronted cupboard with two doors. The whole piece is 4ft 3in (1.30m) wide and 7ft 9in (2.27m) high.

164. An English Mechanical Writing Desk

This extraordinary desk, 3ft 5½in (1.05m) wide, was presented to Princess Alexandra of Denmark by the people of Bath in 1870. It was intended to mark her marriage to the Prince of Wales in 1863, but the sheer complexity of the design and the difficulty in obtaining the materials caused considerable delay. Like many of the presentation and exhibition pieces of the Victorian period it is a virtuoso display of ingenuity and fine workmanship in exotic woods, but typically the overall effect is less than graceful. The four legs are in the form of peacocks carved from solid rosewood, attended by pairs of cherubs carved from limewood. Each bears a different coat-of-arms, for England, Wales, Scotland and Ireland. The sides and the back are mounted with Royal Worcester plaques depicting various episodes in the history of Bath with royal connections. The two shelves in the superstructure are of ivory, supported on ivory columns with ormolu capitals. From the centre of the leather-lined writing surface a counterbalanced ivory stationery compartment rises at the turn of a key to form a slope. Inside it is fitted for letter-writing, with lidded boxes for stamps and an oval looking-glass mounted in the hinged lid.

165. A Mid-19th-Century English Papier Mâché Table Desk

This English piece, 1ft 3in (38cm) wide, is inlaid with mother-of-pearl and decorated with sprigs of flowers and views of castles. The domed lid and double doors of the upper part open to reveal a stationery rack and the shaped front folds forward to become a writing slope.

166. An English Victorian Camphorwood Travelling Secretaire Chest, c1870

Built in two parts, each 2ft 6in (99cm) wide, this desk has flush brass mounts to reinforce the corners and flush brass handles on all the drawers. Chests of this kind, also known as campaign or military chests, were produced in great numbers during the 19th century for soldiers and administrators bound for the colonies. The two box-like sections would probably have been packed into protective pine cases whilst in transit, with the four turned feet unscrewed and stored in one of the drawers.

162

166

165

163

164

Davenports

The davenport was one of the most distinctive types of small desk found in the 19th-century English home. It began as a plain and neat slope-front desk right at the end of the 18th century and survived in a variety of guises, some highly ornate, right up to the end of the 19th century. Several of the variations of the standard form are illustrated here.

167. An English Regency Burr Elm Davenport

This is a slightly ornamented version of the earliest style of plain rectangular davenport which first appeared in the late 18th century. Like them it has a sloping desk top which slides forward when in use to give knee-room, and is quite small, 1ft 8in (51cm) wide, on lobed bun feet and with a turned spindle gallery around the top. It has three drawers with turned ebonised handles on the righthand side and three dummy drawers on the other, with pull-out slides on each side. On the righthand side there is also a small pen drawer.

168. A Satinwood Davenport of the Mid-1820s

This elegant desk retains the little pen drawer in the side found on earlier models; however, the fluted columns with leafy capitals supporting the hinged slope-front make it easier for the writer to sit at the desk and there is no need for a sliding top section. There are four drawers down the righthand side behind a panelled door and the width of this desk is 1ft 8in (51cm).

169. A Rosewood Davenport, Mid-1830s

This example has a sliding top, but the slight overhang of the front and the carved scroll supports hint at the fully detached cabriole supports of the later piano-front davenports.

It is 1ft 11½in (60cm) wide, with four drawers in the side and a hinged leather-lined slope over a satinwood-veneered interior of small drawers.

170. A Typical Victorian Walnut Piano-Front Davenport, c1850

It has leaf-carved scroll supports at the front, four drawers down one side and four dummy drawers down the other and a stationery compartment beneath a hinged top with a fretwork gallery. The hinged piano front folds back to reveal a pull-out writing slide and small drawers. Davenports of this type were made in very large numbers in the mid-Victorian period. This one is 1ft 10in (57cm) wide.

167

169

168

170

171. An English Victorian Papier Mâché Davenport

Because it was light, strong and cheap to produce, papier mâché offered Victorian furniture-makers a free hand in the mass manufacture of highly-decorated pieces. The main centre of production was in the Midlands around Birmingham, where Jennens & Bettridge were the most important firm. Tea trays, small boxes, screens and tables are the most common papier mâché survivors, but larger reminders of this once-thriving industry are more rare.

This example, 2ft 3in (68.5cm) wide, is black japanned and decorated with gilding and mother-of-pearl. The piano-fronted flap is hinged in two places and folds back to reveal a velvet-lined writing slope with drawers and pigeonholes. On the righthand side a small pen drawer can be seen above a cupboard containing two drawers and an arched recess.

172. A Victorian Ebonised Davenport

This compact little desk, 1ft 10in (58cm) wide, is one of many variations on the highly popular davenport pattern, having a two-door cabinet superstructure in the manner of a bonheur-du-jour. The exterior is inset with panels of burr walnut veneer, inlaid with boxwood stringing and mounted with a brass gallery and strips of brass beading along some edges. Here the cabinet is shown opened to reveal the boldly striped veneer of the backs of the doors, the pair of matching drawers with inset handles and the stepped interior of pierced fretwork letter racks. The writing drawer, which contains two brass-topped glass ink bottles and a pen tray, is also open to show the adjustable leather-lined slope. The base contains four drawers down the righthand side, with four matching drawers on the left.

173. A Walnut Davenport of the 1890s

This unusual piece has a square flat top surrounded by a wooden gallery on three sides and supported on a central pedestal. The frieze at the front of the top drops down to reveal a pull-out writing slope in bird's eye maple, fitted with small drawers and a pen tray. The ends of the pedestal are fitted with pierce-carved panels of interlaced ribbon design backed with silk, one of which forms a door which conceals four mahogany-fronted drawers.

172

173

171

174. A Superior Grade Example of Wooton's Patent Desk

In the picture, the desk, 4ft (1.22m) wide, is shown closed to display the richness of its architectural ornament and open to reveal the complexity of the storage compartments inside.

This type of desk was manufactured at William S. Wooton's factory at Indianapolis in the late 19th century and was very popular with businessmen. It was available in four grades (this example is particularly heavily ornamented) but each grade worked on the same basic principle. The front is divided vertically into two sections, one fitted with a letterbox for messages when the desk is closed. These sections swing out on castors, so that anyone sitting at the fold-down writing surface is effectively surrounded by pigeonholes and drawers of every shape and size. As a practical work-centre the Wooton Patent Desk is unrivalled, even by the most lavishly fitted bureau-cabinets of the early 18th century. It is also a supreme example of Victorian igenuity and eclectic ornamentation.

175. An American Late-19th Century Extra Grade Walnut Cylinder Desk.

This is another type of desk patented by Wooton, less well-known than the larger double-doored examples but made with characteristic attention to detail. It is fitted with a pull-out writing slide and the base pedestals contain drawers which swing open to reveal the extensive filing compartments.

174

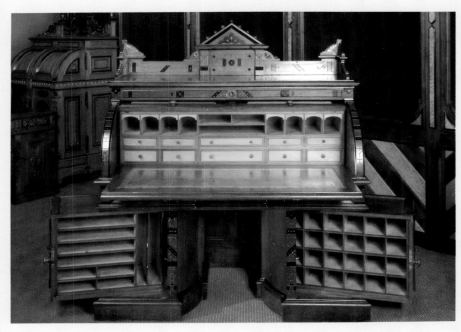

175

176. An American Victorian Painted Pine 'Cottage' Desk-and-Bookcase, c1860

The piece is in three sections, comprising a glazed bookcase with a wide, overhanging cornice, a slope-front writing compartment fitted with drawers and pigeonholes, and one long drawer overhanging a base of three graduated drawers. "Cottage" furniture was a mid-19th century fashion in the USA; it was cheaply constructed in factories but could be richly painted to brighten even the humblest home. This desk was manufactured by the Heywood Brothers of Gardner, Massachusetts, and is a very superior example of the type, and is thought to have been decorated by Edward and Thomas Hill, two English brothers who later gained fame as landscape painters. Their work is evident here in the landscape vignettes on the slope front, the sides and the bottom drawer.

177. Two Examples of the Revival of Sheraton style

This revival took place in England at the end of the 19th century. The 4ft (1.22m)-wide Carlton House desk, which is of satinwood inlaid throughout with delicate neo-classical ornament, is a faithful echo of similar desks made a century before. This tiny sycamore slope-front lady's desk, which is only 1ft 5in (43cm) wide, follows the Sheraton style with its delicate tapering legs, boxwood stringing and inlaid roundel, but it is not of a design so often associated with the Sheraton period. The top is hinged and inside there is a velvet writing slope with bottle wells and a pen tray, while the frieze holds a single drawer.

176

177

1800-1900

178. An English Oak Cabinet and Desk, 1862

This massive piece of furniture was decorated by the architect John Pollard Seddon and decorated by Morris, Marshall, Faulkner & Co in 1862. The central sloping section lifts and tilts on a double ratchet in the same way as the top of an architect's table and beneath it are small shelves and drawers for storing papers. The paintings on the main panels represent an allegory of the arts, symbolised by episodes from the honeymoon of René of Anjoy, and were executed by Ford Madox Brown, Danté Gabriel Rossetti and Edward Burne-Jones, all of whom were members of the firm founded by William Morris in an attempt to restore Medieval values to the applied arts. Morris, the founding father of the Arts and Crafts movement, was reacting against the mass-production of furnishings in the Victorian period and advocated honest craftsmanship, carried out by a contented craftsman for the use and pleasure of the community. This consciously Medieval desk illustrates the two contradictory sides of the movement: simple, undisguised construction (which was to influence 20th century designers) is combined with a chivalric idealism. Morris's furniture was always a luxury product, way beyond the means of the ordinary people he wished to serve.

179. An American Sycamore Writing Cabinet on Stand

This was designed by George Jack for Morris & Co in 1893. Jack was an American-born architect who joined Morris as chief furniture designer, giving an 18th century feel to many of the pieces produced in the 1890s. This writing cabinet, which has a central fall front flanked by cupboards, is very different in style from the painstakingly Gothic furniture produced by Morris and his associates in the infancy of the Arts and Crafts Movement. It is 4ft 7½in (1.41m) wide, decorated with a marquetry design of oak and ash leaves, thistles and other stylised foliage.

180

178

179

181

180. A Late-19th Century English Oak Writing Desk

This desk was designed by the leading English architect and designer Charles Voysey. It has a single cupboard in the upper section with decorative copper hinges and a simple fold-out writing surface. Voysey was influenced by William Morris but he developed a personal style in furniture design, frequently incorporating pierce-decorated hinges, as here. He influenced the designs of Charles Rennie Mackintosh and was one of the first to appreciate the importance of functional industrial design.

181. An English Oak Writing Desk Designed by Arthur Heygate Mackmurdo and made by the Century Guild, c1886

The first successful craft co-operative, the Century Guild was set up by Mackmurdo in 1882 with the aim of rendering 'all branches of art the sphere no longer of the tradesman but of the artist'. Mackmurdo was an architect by training but, having come under the influence of John Ruskin, he proved better than Ruskin at putting ideals of co-operative craftsmanship into practice. He succeeded in uniting artists from the traditionally separate disciplines of architecture, interior design and decoration, and the guild flourished until 1888.

182. A Late 19th-or Early 20th-Century Marquetry Cylinder Bureau

A high-quality reproduction after a Riesener original of the late 18th century, it has a fitted interior beneath the cylinder and a pull-out writing slide with a leather lining, over three frieze drawers. It is 3ft 8½in (1.13m) wide. There is an oval flower marquetry panel at the centre of the cover and the mounts are of a good standard. This elegant and practical writing desk is of a pattern particularly favoured by Paris *ébénistes* during the late 19th century.

183. 'La Forêt Lorraine', 1889

This carved walnut bureau was made in Emile Gallé's factory at Nancy in the west of France and exhibited at the *Exposition Universelle* in Paris.

Although he was a leading figure in the Art Nouveau movement, Gallé tended to avoid the extremes of organic form in his furniture design, and this little desk is wholly traditional in its basic shape. Gallé revitalised the craft of marquetry, using a wide variety of fruitwoods and exotic woods to create beautiful, intricate inlays. The inspiration for these marquetry designs came from the countryside of Lorraine. Gallé was a knowledgeable botanist, and his favourite themes were local plants including cow-parsley, water lilies, orchids and irises, with insects such as dragonflies and butterflies. There was a strong link between the decorative arts and literature at this time, and Gallé often inscribed his furniture with quotations from Hugo, Verlaine and other contemporary poets in order to endow the work with greater significance. He sometimes also gave names to his pieces, in the manner of paintings or music, this desk being an example.

185

182

184

183

184. A French Mahogany, Oak and Walnut Writing Desk, *c*1900

This desk was made at Louis Marjorelle's factory in Nancy. It has a central letter rack flanked by small drawers and an undertier shaped at the front to accommodate the writer's legs.

Majorelle trained as a painter but then concentrated on running his father's furniture business in Nancy, making 18th-century reproduction furniture. During the 1890s, he began to emulate the organic, sinuous forms of the Art Nouveau furniture produced by Emile Gallé's factory, which was also in Nancy. By the time this desk was made, Majorelle was the biggest supplier of Art Nouveau furniture in France, making use of mechanized workshops to turn out high-quality pieces of good design.

185. A North Italian Bureau-Cabinet, *c*1900

The decoration on this desk is a combination of neo-rococo and Japanese-inspired elements, painted over in cream and gold. The upper doors are decorated with a crane, ducks and reeds, and the base doors with Japanese figures dancing and playing music in a landscape. Between the two is a shaped-front secretaire drawer. The whole piece is 3ft 9in (1.20m) wide.

1900
TO
1988

Employees at work in the mailing department of the office building designed for S.C. Johnson & Son at Racine, Wisconsin, by Frank Lloyd Wright. The distinctive round-ended desks, manufactured by Steelcase, were also designed by Wright, who was one of the first to match the design of the office itself with a fully developed range of desks for different uses within the organisation.

The beginning of this century saw a great variety of furniture styles vying for fashionable acceptance in America and Europe, and the writing desk, now an essential part of a well-appointed home, was found in many different guises, but the well-tried solutions of the past – fall-fronts, fitted drawers and pull-out slides – were generally retained even when the overall style was avant garde.

Art Nouveau was one of the most widely disseminated of the international styles and it continued to exert an influence in the first decade of the century. The style had emerged in Continental Europe in the 1880s as a conscious attempt to create something new to replace the worn-out revivals that dominated the salon furniture of the time.

Inspiration came from sinuous natural forms and at its best Art Nouveau furniture has an easy, flowing quality which masks the difficulties of its construction. By the turn of the century it was being produced in large quantities by makers like Emile Gallé and Louis Majorelle in France, but ultimately it was not suited to mass production and it became one of the many casualties of the First World War.

Function rather than form was to be the springboard for 20th century furniture design, but it was not until the 1920s that this concept was fully developed. Nevertheless the years before the First World War were a time for experiment; designers like Charles Rennie Mackintosh in British and Joseph Hoffman and Koloman Moser in Austria produced some highly individual furniture which was stylistically influential without being functionally revolutionary.

It should not be assumed that all new furniture of the early 20th century was modern in its styling. Just as the Victorians had bought faithful reproductions of earlier styles (some so faithful they found their way into museum collections without detection), the Edwardians commissioned many fine pieces in Sheraton and Adam style, and these fashionable revivals were reflected in commercially produced ranges.

Throughout this century writing desks have continued to be made in antique styles or approximations to them. Such imitation can be seen as an endorsement of the functional designs of earlier craftsmen but it is also a reflection on the status of the writing desk as an accepted, even as an increasingly old-fashioned item of furniture, for it is the novelties of an age – radios and refrigerators being 20th century examples – that tend to attract the most distinctive and progressive styling.

The cocktail cabinet was one of the typical forms of the post First World War years, when the restrained, sleek look that had already been evident in some of the work of Hoffman and Moser came to the notice of a wider public.

This new style, which has since come to be known as Art Deco, a name derived from the *Exposition Internationale des Arts Décoratifs et Industriels Modernes* held in Paris in 1925, promoted a sumptuous low-slung look in interior design, intensified by large expanses of gleaming veneer, exotic materials like shark skin and crackle lacquer, and bright chrome and steel.

During a period of economic depression, when cinema provided the dreams, many of the most public manifestations of Art Deco, as in the interior decoration of the French luxury liners *Ile de France* (1927) and *Normandie* (1932), produced a grand but slightly unreal atmosphere reminiscent of a film set. Such opulence did not come cheaply and the overall effect was in any case much more suited to the studies and offices of business tycoons than to the ordinary home or the typing pool.

The chrome and steel used to sensuous effect in the more luxurious Art Deco pieces was, however, an acknowledgement of a parallel movement in furniture design which made more use of the inherent strength of modern materials like plywood, tubular steel and sheet metal.

Functionalism had its philosophical roots in the 18th century but it was in the 20th century that the idea that beauty could be directly equated with fitness for purpose began to have a dramatic effect on furniture design. It was first taken up by architects like Louis Sullivan and Frank Lloyd Wright in America before the First World War and later in Europe by Le Corbusier, whose famous description of a house as 'a machine for living in' automatically extended to the way in which it was furnished.

Generally, though, it was not the home that was most affected but the office, itself an increasingly important aspect of modern life, complicated by the advent of teleprinter, telephone and typewriter.

Frank Lloyd Wright's sheet metal desks designed for the Larkin Building in Buffalo, New York, in 1904 were an early intimation of the shape of things to come, just as his more aesthetically pleasing wood and tubular steel desks designed for the Johnson Wax office in Wisconsin in the late 1930s prefigured the post Second World War designer desk systems.

In Europe one of the leading influences in functional design was the Bauhaus, a craft school founded by the German architect Walter Gropius at Weimar in 1919. The school survived only until 1933, but it established design standards that were adapted to machine production and spawned a generation of utilitarian office furniture that was very obviously modern.

The Second World War set in its own limitations on furniture design, just as the Great War had done, and in Britain it led to government intervention in the furniture industry, so that only approved designs could be manufactured between 1943 and 1952. The 'Utility' furniture that resulted – plain, unpretentious, but of guaranteed minimum quality – was intended to help the re-furnishing of bombed-out homes, it also helped to establish the idea that utility and good design were not mutually exclusive.

The rapid technological developments since the Second World War have resulted in a decline in the importance of desks in the home, with a correspondingly increased interest in the design of office furniture, with all the attendant problems of paper storage, lines of communication through large organisations and working environment.

The image of the office as an arena for modern design has been strengthened in the 1970s and '80s by the growing importance of computers for information storage and communication. Apart from the need to house and use the machines themselves the new technology has also posed problems in the management of electrical cables on a large scale.

Various approaches have been tried, including modular systems which incorporate the electrical equipment in a uniform office environment, 'Hi-Tech' systems which emphasise the structural aspects of the new technology and flexible 'non-systems' which create a less formal working atmosphere.

Whatever the approach, it has been necessary to rethink the way in which workspace is used and there are almost certainly more dramatic solutions on the horizon.

Faced with the welter of cables and the loom of the visual display unit, the traditional desk has retreated, but only as far as the offices of senior management, where a large and imposing antique desk has always added respectability to power.

186. An American Oak Desk, *c*1900

This large piece was designed by Frank Lloyd Wright for a house at Kankakee, Illinois. Its broad overhanging top is 7ft 8in (2.34m) long, supported on two pedestals of three drawers each.

Wright is remembered as one of the most influential architects of the 20th century; he also took great care in commissioning furniture to fill the rooms of the homes he designed. Wright generally made use of massive rectangular forms, carefully balanced one against another, and was influenced, both in choice of material and simplicity of design, by the work of Arts and Crafts furniture makers.

187. An American Oak Fall-Front Writing Cabinet, *c*1902

This was designed by the architect Frank Lloyd Wright for the house he created for Francis W. Little at Peoria, Illinois. It is 5ft 9in (1.76m) high but only 1ft 9in (54cm) wide and seems to have been intended to stand on one side of a fireplace in the master bedroom, complemented by a similarly-proportioned cabinet on the other side. The mirrored door at the top opens to reveal shelves and the flap below it drops down to provide a working surface with pigeonholes behind. In the base there are five drawers. The whole is neat and sedate, designed to fit in with Wright's decorative scheme for the house.

188. A Painted Steel Office Desk, 1904

Wright again designed furniture to match the building that was to house it, and this set was designed for the administration building of the Larkin mail order company at Buffalo, New York. Wright's air-conditioned building, with its central open hall lit by skylights, was an avant garde design that was matched by equally innovative office furniture. The metal desks were built with efficiency in mind; there are banks of pigeonholes for filing along the back and an integral swivel chair without legs which can easily be pushed back and forth to make office cleaning easier. This design set a precedent for the use of metal furniture and for the creation of a single system for the entire office, which were to become standard later in the century.

187

186

188

189. An American Oak Fall-Front Desk with Iron Handles

2ft 6 in (81cm) wide, c1910, a typical plank-constructed product of the Stickley workshops.

Gustav Stickley was one of the most practical and successful of the American exponents of the Arts and Crafts ideal. He began his career making furniture in a variety of fashionable revivalist styles, but he took the writings of English Arts and Crafts pioneers to heart and set about putting his ideas into practice after 1898, producing simple plank-constructed pieces with tenon joints and almost no decoration. He showed a common sense that many idealists lack and was happy to use machines in his workshop where it made the work easier and the product cheaper without interfering with quality. The style soon gained the name Mission Furniture, but Stickley wrote in one of his trade catalogues 'I had no idea of attempting to create a new style, but merely tried to make furniture which would be simple, durable, comfortable, and fitted for the place it had to occupy and the work it had to do'. In many ways the American public was more ready than their European counterparts to accept a plain and simple 'non-style' which owed no debt to history and evoked the rugged life of the early settlers. Stickley's *United Craftsmen* company prospered and expanded, but it also attracted competitors and eventually went bankrupt in 1916 having opened large offices and showrooms in New York.

189

190

191

190. An American Leather-Topped Mahogany Library Table

This massively constructed piece, 4ft (1.23m) wide, was made in Gustav Stickley's workshops but is not typical of Stickley's output in that it is made of an exotic hardwood rather than an indigenous wood like oak, but it clearly shows the Stickley trademark on the inside of one of the trestle supports. It is a red transfer consisting of a joiner's compass with Stickley's signature underneath and the motto *Als Ik Kan* (As I Can), a precept taken from the 15th-century Flemish artist Jan van Eyck, in the centre.

191. An American Oak Fall-Front Desk, *c*1904

The panelled fall is inlaid with stylised motifs in pewter and various light woods and conceals an interior with a central drawer surrounded with shelves and pigeonholes. The exterior has been darkened by fuming, a favourite Stickley finish, while the interior is made of much lighter wood. This desk was designed by Harvey Ellis, who worked for Stickley for a period before his death in 1904 and introduced his characteristic inlaid ornament to the company's range. It is 2ft 6in (76cm) wide.

192. A Scottish Ebonised Oak, Mother-of-Pearl, Metal and Glass Writing Cabinet, 1904

This writing cabinet, 3ft (92cm) wide, was made for the study of the Scottish architect Charles Rennie Mackintosh to his own design. Here the desk is shown open to reveal pigeonholes and shelves over the writing surface, with an open folio stand below. The stark angular design, relieved by the sparkle of small pieces of glass and mother-of-pearl, is typical of Mackintosh's work, as is the distinctive glass and metal flower panel at the centre of the cabinet.

The desk is a copy of one originally designed for the home of Glasgow publisher Walter Blackie, Hill House, which was one of Mackintosh's most important domestic architectural commissions. His highly individual furniture forms were both influenced by and a reaction against the products of the Arts and Crafts movement and were more influential on the Continent than in Britain. In Austria designers like Hoffman and Moser showed a similarly angular response to the curves of the Art Nouveau style.

193. An English Writing Cabinet Veneered in Ebony and Holly

This beautiful piece of furniture, 4ft 5in (1.35m) high, with decorative painting and fittings and mounts of wrought iron and silver, was designed by Charles Robert Ashbee in 1902.

Ashbee was a leading figure in the British Arts and Crafts Movement in the late 19th century, and founder of the Guild and School of Handicraft at Toynbee Hall in the East End of London in 1888. Ashbee followed the basic tenets of the movement in encouraging undivided labour, with each craftsman involved in every stage of production. Like many other pioneers, however, Ashbee found it difficult to compete with commercial firms and after a move to the Cotswolds in 1902, his venture folded in 1914.

195

192

193

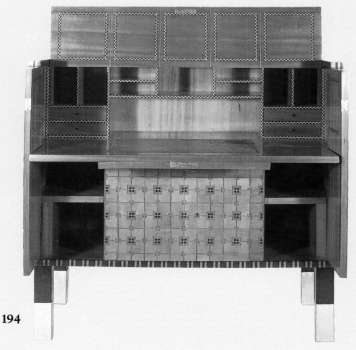

194

194. An Austrian Secessionist Desk, 1902

1900-1988

This piece, designed by the Viennese designer Koloman Moser and made of elm, ivory, mother of pearl, ebony and jacaranda, was a special commission for the Chateâu Charlottenlund near Stockholm.

It is 3ft 11in (1.20m) wide. Here it is shown open for use, and the design appears sober and symmetrical. However, when the fall-front is lifted and the two doors closed it reveals a restrained exoticism typical of the avant-garde Viennese artists of the time. The whole of the front is inlaid with a parquetry pattern of interlocking squares and the centre of the fall-front is decorated with a pair of mother-of-pearl maidens holding inlaid brass rings and flanked by stylised dolphins in ebony.

Koloman Moser was one of a group of artists (including Joseph Hoffmann, Otto Wagner, Josef Olbrich and Gustav Klimt) who broke away from the conservative Vienna Academy in 1897. The Secessionist Exhibition Gallery was opened in 1898 and in 1903 Moser and Hoffman founded the Wiener Werkstätte, a craft co-operative producing metalware, furniture and textiles. Although the Werkstätte was based on the Arts and Crafts guilds set up in Britain, the rigorous rectilinear designs of the early years were closer to the work of the Glasgow designer Charles Rennie Mackintosh than to the mainstream Arts and Crafts products or the Art Nouveau creations seen elsewhere in Europe, which relied on organic forms and sinuous curves.

195. An English Holly and Ebony Veneered Desk, 1916

The desk, which is 2ft 3in (99cm) wide, with five drawers in the front and a simple superstructure, was designed by Roger Fry at the Omega Workshops in London. It was part of a commission to furnish an entire apartment for the wife of the Belgian ambassador, Lalla Vandervelde, with the distinctive brightly painted pieces produced by Fry and the young artists who worked with him. The desk was the only marquetry piece in the commission, but it shows some of the signs of careless craftsmanship (badly fitting drawers and poor-quality marquetry) typical of the workshop, which was set up in 1913, partly as a reaction to the serious Craft Guild mentality of the post-Morris era. Fry was more concerned with spontaneity and artistic expression than with craftsmanship and technique, but he did provide many keen young artists with a means of earning a living, and by cultivating clients he managed to see the workshop through the difficult period of the First World War, finally closing it down in 1919.

196. A French Black Lacquer Art Deco Kneehole Desk and Chair, *c*1925

The desk was designed by Jean Dunand and Serge Revinski, and is 3ft 11in (1.19m) wide, with four drawers in each pedestal. The hinged central writing slope is covered with lozenges of shagreen and the top of each pedestal is hinged to give access to a compartment beneath.

Dunand was born in Switzerland and while working in Paris he learned the correct oriental technique for lacquering from the Japanese artist Sugawara. The smooth lines and surfaces of Dunand's furniture designs are among the most distinctive of the Inter-War years.

198

199

197. A French Half-Round Pedestal Desk

This unusual and attractive piece was designed as a special commission by Jacques-Emile Ruhlmann. The top is fitted with five double-hinged compartments radiating from a leather writing surface with two cut-glass inkwells. The left-hand pedestal is fitted with drawers with gilt bronze handles and the right-hand with a tambour shutter over a drawer. Both stand on gilt bronze pedestals joined by a gilt bronze stretcher. The distinctive striped veneer is macassar ebony, an exotic wood much favoured by Art Deco furniture designers for its sleek, dramatic appearance.

Ruhlmann was the leading Parisian interior decorator of the 1920s, producing very expensive but beautifully made furniture, much of which bears his mark.

198. A French Art Deco Pedestal Desk Veneered in Rosewood, by Jules Leleu, c1930

There are drawers in each end of the large pedestal and on one side of each of the smaller pedestals. The three-way design is unusual, but the clean straight lines, the use of rich, figured veneer in wide expanses and chromium-plated handles and bases are typical of the best quality Art Deco furniture. The whole construction measures 6ft 3¾in (1.92m) across.

199. A French Desk, c1928

This beautiful desk in Brazilian jacaranda, ivory and chromed steel was designed by the French architect and interior decorator Pierre Chareau. Chareau was one of the leading designers of the Art Deco movement. He produced luxurious, highly finished interiors, but also gave thought to the practical design of desks of all kinds. Here the very simple central section is flanked by a pair of swinging drawers with ivory escutcheons on one side and on the other side by a nest of four tables which expand on a central hinge to provide the writer with extra space. The tables can be separated from the desk and used on their own.

Jacaranda was a veneer popular with French cabinetmakers in the 1920s due to its rich and distinctive grain.

196

197

200. A British Double Architect's Desk and Matching Chair, 1935

This set of painted tubular steel and painted wood was made by by the British firm PEL (Practical Equipment Ltd). The desk has a single long frieze drawer and three smaller drawers suspended in the framework. It is attached to an adjustable drawing board, giving an overall width of 9ft (2.75m).

By the mid-1930s British firms were following the Continental lead in exploiting the strength, economy and clean modern lines of bent tubing. The principal European producer was the Vienna-based firm of Thonet. Having pioneered the mass manufacture of inexpensive bentwood furniture as early as the 1830s, they adapted naturally to the new materials, which had a similar combination of strength and flexibility.

201. An American Desk and Chair, 1936–39

This set was a standard piece designed for the administration building Wright conceived for the Johnson Wax Company at Racine, Wisconsin. The dynamic curving lines of this furniture echo the shape of the building itself. The desk consists of three round-edged worktops of polished American walnut overhanging a frame of red enamelled steel with semi-circular swing-out steel drawers. This was the basic module; Wright designed many variation for different applications throughout the building. His thoughtful creation of a modular system that was efficient and reflected the style of the building that housed what must have been the envy of many later designers. His attitude to seating was as revolutionary as his architecture – three-legged chairs encourage good posture: if you don't sit up you fall over.

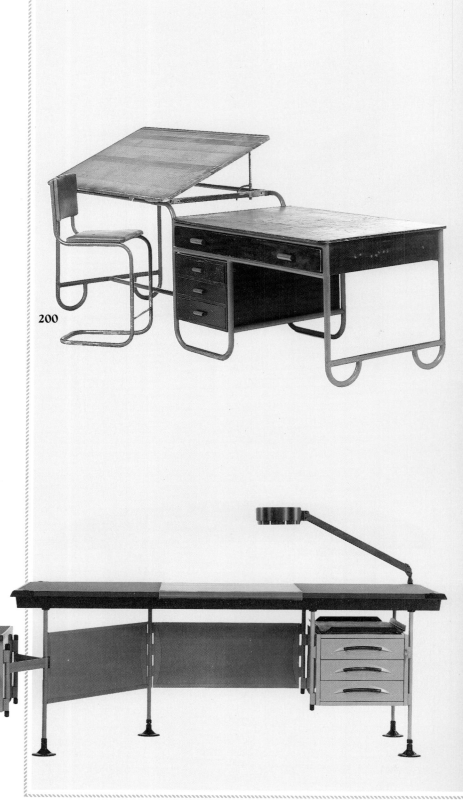

200

204

203

201

202. A French Leather and Glass Desk, early 1950s

The 6ft 11in (2.10m) wide top is of boomerang form in thick red glass, supported on tubular metal legs sewn into a black leather covering, with a magazine rack on the left and two swivel drawers on the right. For an important commission this designer has used modern materials but softened the stark lines and spindly supports of typical 1950s office furniture with leather padding by Hermès.

It was designed by Jacques Adnet for the president of a French aviation company.

203. An Italian Oak Two-tier Desk of the Mid-1950s

It is stamped *Silvio Cavatorta, Roma*, but its stylish design clearly shows the influence of one of the greatest Italian designers of the period, Carlo Mollino. Supported on two K-frames, the top tier serves as a working surface over a shelf, with two angled double-drawer units below. It is 5ft 7in (1.7m) wide.

204. An Italian Office Desk of Tubular and Sheet Steel, Vinyl and Cloth

This whole concept is made up from modules of the *Spazio* system launched by Olivetti in 1961. Olivetti produced a series of standard modules that could be manufactured cheaply because they required little complicated welding or fitting, but which could be made up in a variety of combinations by the customer to fit any office or application. This is an early and stylish example of the trend towards factory-produced DIY furniture, which today is seen at its most developed in the domestic fitted kitchen.

202

119

Monarchs

The names of English and French monarchs are often used to denote the period of a piece of furniture when the precise date of manufacture is not known.

In some cases a ruler is closely associated with a recognisable style; Louis XIV, for instance, saw the development of the decorative arts in France as a matter of policy and the massive formal designs of his time reflect the elaboration of life at his court. Dramatic upheavals such as the French Revolution brought about dramatic changes in style but generally changes of style were gradual and overlapped the reigns of different monarchs.

In Britain especially, the machinery of fashion tended to be more loosely linked to the sovereign and public taste was influenced by a variety of factors. This was especially true during the reign of long-lived monarchs like George III (1760-1820) and the names of the producers of cabinetmakers' pattern books, like Chippendale, Sheraton and Hepplewhite are often used quite freely to denote the style of their times. These cabinetmakers were influential not necessarily because of their designs but because they recorded contemporary styles, some of which of course may have been their own.

American furniture periods tend to be classified using a mixture of English monarchs and makers, and the dating is complicated by the fact that it took a long time for European styles to cross the Atlantic so that the American period occurs several years behind the corresponding period in Britain. For example, Queen Anne died in 1714, but the American Queen Anne style is taken to cover the period 1720-1750.

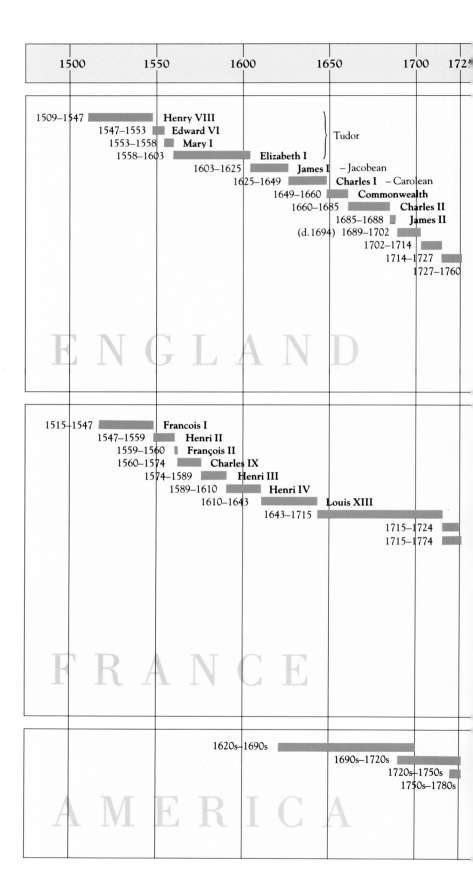

ENGLAND

1500	1550	1600	1650	1700	1725

1509–1547 Henry VIII
1547–1553 Edward VI
1553–1558 Mary I
1558–1603 Elizabeth I
} Tudor
1603–1625 James I – Jacobean
1625–1649 Charles I – Carolean
1649–1660 Commonwealth
1660–1685 Charles II
1685–1688 James II
(d.1694) 1689–1702
1702–1714
1714–1727
1727–1760

FRANCE

1515–1547 Francois I
1547–1559 Henri II
1559–1560 François II
1560–1574 Charles IX
1574–1589 Henri III
1589–1610 Henri IV
1610–1643 Louis XIII
1643–1715
1715–1724
1715–1774

AMERICA

1620s–1690s
1690s–1720s
1720s–1750s
1750s–1780s

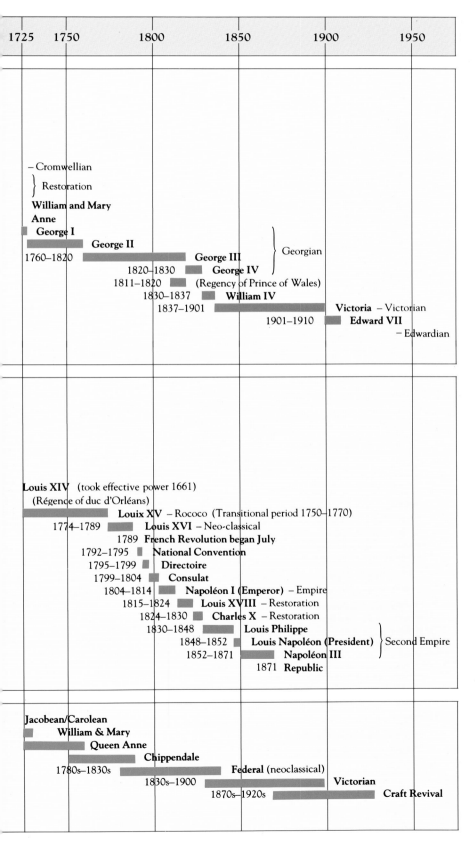

1725   1750   1800   1850   1900   1950

– Cromwellian
} Restoration
William and Mary
Anne
 George I
     George II
1760–1820
          George III   } Georgian
     1820–1830   **George IV**
     1811–1820   (Regency of Prince of Wales)
       1830–1837   **William IV**
        1837–1901   **Victoria** – Victorian
             1901–1910   **Edward VII**
                        – Edwardian

Louis XIV (took effective power 1661)
(Régence of duc d'Orléans)
           Louix XV – Rococo (Transitional period 1750–1770)
1774–1789   **Louis XVI** – Neo-classical
     1789   **French Revolution began July**
1792–1795   **National Convention**
1795–1799   **Directoire**
1799–1804   **Consulat**
1804–1814   **Napoléon I (Emperor)** – Empire
1815–1824   **Louis XVIII** – Restoration
1824–1830   **Charles X** – Restoration
1830–1848   **Louis Philippe**
  1848–1852   **Louis Napoléon (President)** } Second Empire
  1852–1871   **Napoléon III**
      1871   **Republic**

Jacobean/Carolean
   William & Mary
      Queen Anne
        Chippendale
1780s–1830s   **Federal** (neoclassical)
     1830s–1900   **Victorian**
         1870s–1920s   **Craft Revival**

Cabinetmakers' pattern books and other influential publications

Listed here is a selection of books influential both on the furniture makers and designers of their times and on furniture historians.

Stalker and Parker, **Treatise of Japanning and Varnishing**, 1688

Thomas Chippendale, **Gentleman and Cabinet-Maker's Director**, 1754 (2nd edition 1755; 3rd edition 1762)

Ince and Mayhew, **Universal System of Household Furniture**, 1759–1762

Robert Manwaring, **Cabinet and Chair-Maker's Real Friend and Companion** 1765

Robert and James Adam, **Works in Architecture**, 1773–1778 (2nd volume 1779; 3rd volume 1822)

George Hepplewhite, **Cabinet-Maker and Upholsterer's Guide**, 1788

Thomas Shearer, Hepplewhite and others, **Cabinet-Maker's London Book of Prices**, 1788

Thomas Sheraton, **Cabinet-Maker and Upholsterer's Drawing-Book**, 1791–1794

Percier and Fontaine, **Receuil des décorations intérieurs**, 1801 (2nd edition 1812)

Thomas Sheraton, **Cabinet Dictionary**, 1803

Thomas Hope, **Household Furniture and Interior Decoration**, 1807

George Smith, **Collection of Designs for Household Furniture and Interior Decoration**, 1808

Collection of Ornamental Designs after the Antique, 1812

Cabinet Maker and Upholsterer's Guide, 1826

John C. Loudon, **Encyclopaedia of Cottage, Farm and Villa Furniture**, 1833
Augustus W.N. Pugin, **Gothic Furniture in the style of the 15th century**, 1835

The True Principle of Pointed or Christian Architecture, 1841

Bruce Talbert, **Gothic Forms Applied to Furniture**, 1867

Charles Eastlake, **Hints on Household Taste**, 1868

121

acanthus – A classical ornamental device based on the prickly, indented leaves of the acanthus plant, used especially in the capitals of Corinthian and Composite columns.

anthemion – A classical ornament consisting of a band of alternating floral forms based on the honeysuckle flower. A single motif based on the honeysuckle is also called an anthemion.

apron – An ornamental projection below a rail, often shaped and carved.

astragal – A small half-round moulding frequently used for glazing bars.

arcading – A series of round-topped arches, frequently used decoratively, especially on early carved furniture.

ball and claw foot – A foot in the form of a claw clutching a ball, often used in conjunction with a cabriole leg and popular in England and America in 18th century.

banding – Veneer was often used in bands to form decorative borders to the main surface. Crossbanding was cut across the grain, while feather or herringbone banding was cut with the grain at an angle so that two strips laid side by side resembled a feather.

Baroque – A decorative style which originated in Italy and reached its height in the 17th century, characterised by heavy and exuberant forms. Its influence varied from country to country but baroque furniture tends to be sculptural and often architectural in form and is frequently gilded, with human figures, scrolls and shells much in evidence.

beading – A three-dimensional decorative motif in the form of a series of round beads in a single line or a very fine half-round moulding (see cock beading)

Biedermeier – A German term used to denote both the period 1815–1848 and the decorative style popular in Germany, Austria and Scandinavia from the 1820s to the 1840s, which was characterised by solid, unpretentious furniture in light-coloured woods. Biedermeier was a newspaper caricature symbolising the uncultured bourgeoisie.

blockfront – a form of decoration typical of 18th century East Coast America. Mostly found on chests of drawers and bureaux, it consists of three vertical sections carved from the solid wood, the central one being concave and the two on the outside convex.

bombé – A term adopted from the French for the curved and swollen forms characteristic of the rococo style. Hence bombé base, also called a kettle base in America.

bonheur-du-jour – A French term first noted in the 1770s for a small writing table with a shallow superstructure of shelves, drawers or pigeonholes along the rear edge. This type of lady's desk was immensely popular from the mid-18th century onwards, and although the origin of the name is obscure, it may refer to its fashionable status.

boulle – A distinctive form of marquetry decoration making use of metal and other veneers, usually brass and tortoiseshell, to form a rich pattern. It takes its name from André-Charles Boulle, *ébéniste* to Louis XIV, who perfected but did not invent a technique known in Italy since the late 17th century. The method of production, cutting the design from layers of brass and tortoiseshell glued together, resulted in two sets of veneer. One has the pattern in brass against tortoiseshell (known as *première partie*), the second is the other way round (*contre-partie*).

bowfront – the front of a bureau, chest or cabinet which is formed as a single horizontal curve.

breakfront – A term used to describe a piece of furniture where one or more sections project from the main body of the piece.

bureau – The French word for all kinds of writing desks, often further defined, as in bureau plat or bureau à cylindre. The word is derived from *bureé*, a coarse cloth used to cover the writing tables of clerks and secretaries in the Middle Ages. In Britain bureau has come to mean a slope-front writing desk of traditional pattern; but in America it is used to describe a dressing chest, often with a mirror.

bureau à cylindre (secrétaire à cylindre) – A French term for a roll-top desk with either a solid quarter-cylinder or a flexible tambour covering the writing surface and pigeonholes when closed. The type first appeared c1750, largely supplanting the secrétaire en pente.

bureau de dame – A French 19th-century term for a small writing table used by women and which would more likely have been called a *petite table à écrire* in the 18th century. The term is now used to denote all sorts of small, delicate desks, including bureaux en pente.

bureau en pente – see secrétaire en pente.

bureau Mazarin – a 19th-century term for the type of pedestal desk on legs joined by shaped stretchers which was popular in France at the end of the 17th century, sometime after the death in 1643 of Cardinal Mazarin who is not known to have owned a desk of this type. They are frequently decorated with boulle marquetry.

bureau plat – A French term for a flat-topped writing table with drawers in the frieze and sometimes with extra slides and slopes.

burl – The American term for burr.

burr – see veneer.

butler's desk – An American term for a secretaire chest, usually with curved sides. A butler's sideboard has a secretaire drawer in the middle section.

canted – When legs or projecting members are set at an angle to the corner of a piece they are known as canted legs or canted corners.

Carlton House desk – A contemporary term for a D-shaped writing table with a bank of drawers and cupboards following the curve of the back, which was presumably named after the palace of the then Prince of Wales, later George IV. There is no evidence that he ordered such a desk, but the name appears in records as early as the 1790s.

cartonnier – A filing cabinet also known as a *serre-papiers*, introduced in France during the 18th century. Fitted with pigeonholes, the cartonnier could be an independent piece of furniture, or an accessory intended to stand on or at the end of a bureau plat.

cartouche – An ornamental panel, often a stylised shield, which is decorative itself but can also carry an inscription, a monogram or a crest.

caryatid – An architectural motif consisting of a column in the form of a female figure which is also often found on carved furniture and bronze mounts.

castors – small swivelling wheels attached to the bottom of furniture to make it easier to move.

chamfer – A narrow flat surface formed by cutting away the apex of an angle between two surfaces, thus removing the sharp edge. Hence chamfered leg, chamfered stretcher, etc.

chasing – Engraving. Bronze furniture mounts were chased after casting to sharpen the detail before gilding.

ciseleur – A craftsman who used a variety of chisels and other tools to finish bronze mounts once they had been cast by a *fondeur* or founder. After finishing they were usually gilded by a *doreur*. Under the 18th century Paris guild system the *Fondeurs-Ciseleurs* and the *Doreurs* had separate corporations.

cock beading – A very fine half-round moulding applied around the edges of drawer-fronts.

coffre-fort – A French term for the strong-box which was often incorporated into good quality writing desks.

contre-partie – see boulle.

cornice – An architectural term used in the description of furniture for the top moulding of bookcases and other large pieces, many of which were conceived along architectural lines.

cornucopia – A horn of plenty, used decoratively as a shell-like horn overflowing with fruit.

crossbanding – see banding.

desk and bookcase – The 18th century cabinetmakers' term for what would now be called a bureau-bookcase in Britain. Desk and bookcase is still used in the USA, where such pieces are also called secretaries.

doreur – see ciseleur

ébéniste – A French term for a cabinetmaker, – a specialist in veneered furniture, as distinct from a *menuisier* or joiner who specialised in carved pieces like chairs or beds. A maître of the Paris furniture makers' guild (*Corporation des menuisier-ébénistes*) was not bound to specialise, but the distinction was generally observed until the end of the 18th century.

écran à secretaire, écran à pupitre – A firescreen fitted with a shelf or slide at the back for writing. The type appeared in British pattern books in quite sophisticated form as writing fire screens or screen writing tables and enabled a woman to keep her feet warm while protecting her face. Firescreens were also fitted to some bonheurs-du-jour.

écritoire – A French term for a standish, a container designed to stand on a desk and hold inkwells, sandshakers, pens, penknives, perhaps scissors or a bell to summon a servant to take the finished letter. The term is also used for a travelling writing cabinet.

escritoire – An early 18th century English term for a writing desk, now often used to refer to the large fall-front writing desks of the late 17th and early 18th century.

escutcheon – A plate surrounding and protecting a keyhole.

espagnolette – A decorative motif in the form of a female head surrounded by a stylised lace ruff, much favoured as mounts during the *Régence* period.

estampille – The stamp with the name and initials of a *maître ébéniste* which was obligatory on French furniture from about 1750 until the Revolution. The mark was struck with a cold punch rather than branded, although delicate pieces could be signed in ink. Long names were sometimes shortened, as in BRVB for Bernard van Risenburgh, and the marks were usually in an inconspicuous place, often accompanied by the monogram of the *Corporation des Jurés Menuisiers-Ébénistes* – JME conjoined – a quality control mark. Furniture made for the crown did not have to be stamped.

fall-front – The writing flap on a secretaire which also serves to close the desk when not in use.

festoon – A neo-classical decorative motif in the form of a looped garland of flowers, fruit and foliage.

figure – The natural grain patterns of a veneer are known as figuring.

finial – An ornamental projection from the top of a piece of furniture, often a knob, ball, acorn, urn or flame.

fluting – Decoration in the form of shallow, parallel grooves, especially in columns and pilasters or on the legs of furniture.

fondeur – see ciseleur

fretwork – carved geometrical patterns, either in relief or pierced.

frieze – An architectural term for the flat surface beneath a cornice, used loosely to describe flat horizontal members in furniture, especially below table tops and the cornices of case furniture.

gadroon – A form of decorative edging usually in the form of a series of convex curved lobes or repeated spiral ribs resembling ropetwist.

gallery – a miniature railing, often of brass, placed around the edge of a table or desk top to prevent papers and other small objects slipping off.

gilding – The application of gold to the surface of another material. Bronze mounts were frequently gilded to prevent tarnishing, especially in France. Wood was also gilded for decorative effect.

gradin – A French term for a bank of shelves or drawers, either part of a desk or free-standing; hence bureau à gradin.

Gothic – A decorative style based on the pointed arches, cluster columns, spires and other elements of late medieval architecture. Gothic revivals have influenced furniture design at several periods, particularly in Britain in the mid-18th century and again in the mid-19th century.

inlay – Although it is often used to mean marquetry, inlay strictly refers to decorative materials like ivory or ebony set into the surface of solid wood, unlike veneer which covers the whole surface.

japanning – The term used in America and Britain for techniques imitating the Oriental lacquerwork which began to arrive in Europe via the Dutch East India Company in the 17th century.

joinery – Joined furniture is formed of vertical and horizontal members, united by mortice and tenon joints and supporting panels.

lowboy – A late 17th or 18th century American dressing table on legs, sometimes found combined with a slope-front desk.

maître – A mastercraftsman under the Paris guild system, who was entitled to own a workshop and stamp his pieces, having served an apprenticeship and paid the necessary fees. See estampille.

marchand-mercier – Under the Paris guild system marchands-merciers combined the roles of furniture dealers and interior decorators. They were not allowed to run their own workshops but often exerted considerable influence on fashion by acting as intermediaries between customer and craftsman.

marquetry – The use of veneers (woods of different colours, bone, ivory, mother-of-pearl, tortoiseshell, etc.) to form decorative designs like scrolls, flowers, and landscapes. Abstract geometrical patterns formed in the same manner are known as parquetry.

mechanical writing desk – Desks with complicated mechanisms that operated as flaps or shutters were particularly popular in France, where they were known as bureaux à méchanisme.

member – Any of the structural components (rails, uprights, stretchers, etc.) of a piece of joined furniture.

menuisier – see ébéniste.

mortice and tenon joint – The basic method of joining the framework of a piece of furniture. The tenon is a projection (usually a slim rectangle) at the end of a rail which fits exactly into the mortice, a cavity cut into the side of an upright. The tenon is normally secured by dowels.

moulding – A length of wood or other material applied to the surface of a piece of furniture. The shaped section of a moulding is usually made up from a number of curves, and there are various standard types (astragal, ogee, cavetto, ovolo) mostly of architectural origin.

mounts – Decorative motifs, usually of brass or gilt-bronze, fixed to cabinetwork.

neoclassicism – The predominant decorative style of the second half of the 18th century. Based on the restrained use of Greek and Roman architectural form and ornament, it is characterised by a sober, rectilinear emphasis which was a conscious reaction to the exuberance of the rococo.

ormolu – A term of French origin for the gilt bronze mounts used on furniture, especially in France.

panel – A flat surface supported by rails and stiles in joined furniture.

parcel gilt – Gilded in part only.

parquetry – see marquetry

patera – A neo-classical decorative motif, either oval or round, resembling a stylised flower or rosette.

pediment – an architectural term used to describe an arched or triangular surmount to a bookcase or cabinet.

pierced – Carved ornament is described as pierced when the decoration is cut right through the piece, as in fretwork.

pilaster – A shallow column attached to a piece of furniture.

pounce – A fine powder of pulverised sandarac, used to prevent ink spreading on unsized paper; kept in a pounce pot.

première partie – see boulle.

putto (pl. putti) – A naked infant, often winged, used as a decorative motif. Also referred to as a cherub, a cupid and an amoretto.

rail – a horizontal member used in the construction of joined furniture.

reeding – Decoration in the form of parallel ribbing, especially on columns and pilasters or on the legs of furniture.

Renaissance – The rebirth of ancient Roman values in the arts which began in Italy in the 14th century and gradually replaced the Gothic style in most of Europe during the following two and a half centuries. Renaissance designers were inspired by the sculptural and architectural remains of the ancient world and their furniture reflects this in the profusion of carved ornament.

repoussé work – A form of embossed decoration produced by hammering sheet metal from the underside.

rocaille – Stylised and fanciful rock and shell decoration, used by extension to refer to the decorative forms of the rococo.

rococo – A decorative style which spread from France during the first half of the 18th century, characterised by delicate curved outlines, C-scrolls, fantastic organic forms and a tendency towards asymmetry in ornamental details.

sans traverse – A French term for a commode or desk where there are no visible divisions between drawers and decorative motifs can continue uninterrupted.

screen writing table – see écran à secrétaire.

scriptor – A contemporary English term for a writing desk, now used to denote the small fall-front writing cabinets of the late 17th century.

scrutoire – A 17th century English term for a writing desk, probably a corruption of the French escritoire.

secrétaire – A French term often used for all sorts of desk, but originally denoting those where papers and documents could be kept secret, locked away from prying eyes behind a flap, as in the secrétaire à abattant. In Britain a secretaire is a pull-out writing compartment disguised as a drawer with pigeonholes and small drawers behind a fall-front, usually part of a larger piece such as the secretaire-chest and secretaire-bookcase.

sécretaire à abattant – A French term for desk which stands against the wall like a cabinet or cupboard with a large fall-front which is vertical when closed. First made in the 17th century but very popular in the late 18th century. Also known as a secrétaire en armoire.

secrétaire à capucin – A mechanical writing desk similar to the secrétaire or bureau à la Bourgogne.

secrétaire á la bourgogne – A mechanical writing desk which resembles a table à écrire. When in use one half of the top rises vertically to reveal a bank of small drawers and the other hinges forward as a writing surface. Supposedly named after the duc de Bourgogne, who was paralysed and had a mechanical desk made for him by Oeben.

secrétaire à culbute – Another form of mechanical writing table with a rising bank of drawers which swings up on a hinge along its front edge. From the French culbute, somersault. Also called a secrétaire à cabriolet or a secrétaire à bascule.

secrétaire à rideau – A French term for a tambour desk.

secrétaire en armoire – see secrétaire à abattant.

secrétaire en dos d'ane – A French term often used indiscriminately to refer to all sorts of slope-front desk (secrétaires en pente), but more correctly describing the secrétaire à double pente with two flaps, at which two people can write facing one another.

secrétaire en pente – A French term for a free-standing slope-front desk with a flap which serves as a lid when closed and a writing surface when open.

secretary – A modern American term for desk and bookcase.

serpentine – In the form of an undulating curve, convex at the centre and concave on each side.

serre-papiers – see cartonnier.

stile – A vertical member used in the construction of joined furniture.

strapwork – A form of decoration particularly popular in Northern Europe in the 16th and 17th centuries, resembling interlaced, pierced and scrolled bands of leather.

stretcher – A horizontal crosspiece used to join and strengthen the legs of a piece of furniture.

stringing – Thin strips of wood or metal inlay used to decorate furniture.

strung border – A border decorated with stringing.

swag – A decorative motif in the form of a loop of cloth and similar to a festoon.

table à écrire – A French term denoting a writing table, generally smaller than a bureau plat and provided with a slope or slides and a fitted writing drawer.

table ambulante – An 18th century French term for any light, portable table, usually intended for writing.

table en chiffonière – A small 18th century French work with a high gallery around the top and several drawers in the frieze, often fitted with a writing drawer or slide.

tambour desk – A desk where the writing compartment is hidden behind vertical slatted shutters when not in use (see also roll-top desk).

Vernis martin – A generic name for all varnish and lacquers (japanning) used in France in imitation of oriental lacquer, but specifically referring to the four Martin brothers, who were granted a monopoly on imitation relief lacquer in 1730, which was renewed in 1744.

vitruvian scroll – A classically-derived ornamental device in the form of a series of scrolls resembling waves.

x-frame – An arrangement of diagonal stretchers joining the front and back legs of a piece of furniture and crossing to form an X.

x-stretcher – see x-frame.

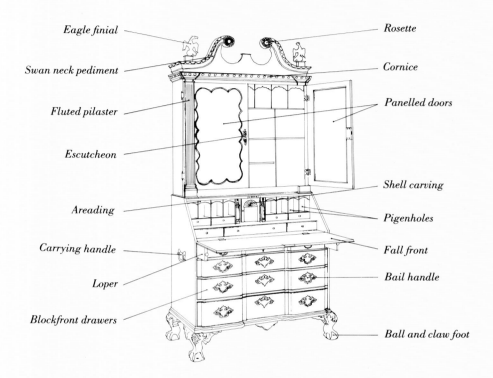

Eagle finial

Swan neck pediment

Fluted pilaster

Escutcheon

Areading

Carrying handle

Loper

Blockfront drawers

Rosette

Cornice

Panelled doors

Shell carving

Pigenholes

Fall front

Bail handle

Ball and claw foot

AMERICAN CHIPPENDALE DESK
AND BOOKCASE, BOSTON C.1760

Leather lined top

Mask

Chutes

Sabot

Scroll toe

Branch and leaf
handles

Frieze drawers

Cabriole leg

EARLY LOUIS XV BUREAU PLAT
WITH ORMOLU MOUNTS, PARIS C.1730'S.

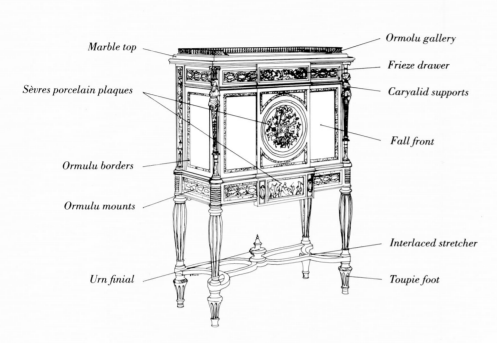

Marble top

Sèvres porcelain plaques

Ormulu borders

Ormulu mounts

Urn finial

Ormolu gallery

Frieze drawer

Caryalid supports

Fall front

Interlaced stretcher

Toupie foot

FRENCH LOUIS XVI SECRETAIRE À ABATTANT
WITH ORMOLU AND PORCELAIN MOUNTS, PARIS C.1785

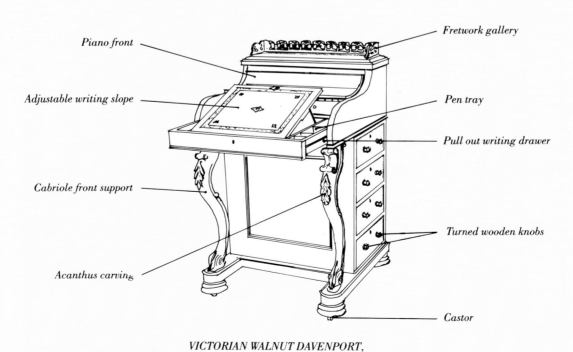

Piano front

Adjustable writing slope

Cabriole front support

Acanthus carving

Fretwork gallery

Pen tray

Pull out writing drawer

Turned wooden knobs

Castor

*VICTORIAN WALNUT DAVENPORT,
ENGLAND C.1860*